CHARLES II'S FAVOURITE MISTRESS

To my Mum and Nan – my own pretty, witty ladies!

CHARLES II'S FAVOURITE MISTRESS

PRETTY, WITTY NELL GWYN

SARAH-BETH WATKINS

PEN & SWORD HISTORY

AN IMPRINT OF PEN & SWORD BOOKS LTD.
YORKSHIRE - PHILADELPHIA

First published in Great Britain in 2021 by
PEN AND SWORD HISTORY
An imprint of
Pen & Sword Books Ltd
Yorkshire – Philadelphia

ISBN 978 1 39900 056 7

Typeset in Times New Roman 11.5/14 by
SJmagic DESIGN SERVICES, India.
Printed and bound by CPI Group (UK) Ltd, Croydon, CR0 4YY

Pen & Sword Books Limited incorporates the imprints of Atlas, Archaeology,
Aviation, Discovery, Family History, Fiction, History, Maritime, Military,
Military Classics, Politics, Select, Transport, True Crime, Air World,
Frontline Publishing, Leo Cooper, Remember When, Seaforth Publishing,
The Praetorian Press, Wharncliffe Local History, Wharncliffe Transport,
Wharncliffe True Crime and White Owl.

For a complete list of Pen & Sword titles please contact
PEN & SWORD BOOKS LIMITED
47 Church Street, Barnsley, South Yorkshire, S70 2AS, England
E-mail: enquiries@pen-and-sword.co.uk
Website: www.pen-and-sword.co.uk

Or
PEN AND SWORD BOOKS
1950 Lawrence Rd, Havertown, PA 19083, USA
E-mail: Uspen-and-sword@casematepublishers.com
Website: www.penandswordbooks.com

Contents

Introduction

Nell Gwyn is the best remembered of Charles II's mistresses, that merry monarch whose restoration to the throne ushered in a new era in English history after years of civil war. There were other women in his life, including his queen, but none of them captured the hearts of the people as Nell did. She was their darling – a commoner raised from the dingy back alleys of London to the stage and into a king's arms. Hers was a true 'rags to riches' story that spoke to the common people. She was one of their own and she gave hope and light to them in their darkest hours. If a street-hawking, ale-serving slip of a girl could rise from the slums of London to grace the court at Whitehall, there was a promise of better days for them all.

And Charles II loved her for never being anything other than her true self. Loved her for her wit and charm, loved her for her mischievous personality and for never giving up her down-to-earth ways. She made him laugh out loud with her antics, brightened the dullness of gloomy days and was a welcome reprieve from royal duty. In time, her house would become his sanctuary, and she was his comfort and solace. She demanded little and gave him everything, including two sons.

Born during the tumultuous times of the English Civil War that ended with the unprecedented death of the reigning monarch, Charles I, Nell's early years – her birthplace, date and even her father – are shrouded in mystery although she would grow up in Restoration London and be proud to call it home.

It was a time of licentiousness, new freedoms, debauchery, scandal and intrigue. But it was also an age of war, plague and fire. Londoners would fear Dutch invasion and hear the booms of naval battle out at sea, die in their thousands from a pestilential disease that ran rife through the city, and lose their homes and livelihoods in the Great Conflagration – occurrences captured by some of the greatest diarists of the age, Samuel Pepys, John Evelyn and John Aubrey.

INTRODUCTION

Nell lived in a time of change and was one of the first English actresses to grace the stage, after Charles II signed probably one of the most significant patents in theatrical history. She rose from selling oranges in the pit and running messages to becoming a successful comedian whom audiences flocked to see, known for her wit, her madcap parts and energetic jigs. Her career spanned seven years, cut short only by her affair with the king, yet the theatre stayed in her heart for the rest of her life.

She wasn't the only woman to become the King's mistress, but she was – and is – the most fondly remembered. Whereas people begrudged the money-grabbing antics of Barbara Villiers, Duchess of Cleveland, and the political machinations of Louise de Keroualle, Duchess of Portsmouth, Londoners were always on Nell's side. She was one of them, their 'Protestant whore', but she was also friends with the foremost peers in the country – men like the Duke of Buckingham and the Earl of Rochester, members of the king's merry gang, notorious in their own ways.

Nell lived a vibrant life surrounded by people she loved and who loved her in return. She embraced the Restoration era and its king with open arms. Nell would share his bed for seventeen years and Charles II would die making sure she would be cared for. But life would never be the same for the pretty, witty actress, and in her final years she remained faithful to her king's memory as she had remained faithful to him in life.

But who was Nell really? She was such a colourful character and there are hundreds of stories about her, making it hard to sift fact from fiction. There are so many tales we would like to believe are genuine but are pure inventions. I hope I have gone some way in finding out the truth although there are some things about Nell we will never know for definite, and so much more we can only guess at.

This book will look at the contradicting stories of her early life, from her birth date to birthplace, her role as one of England's first actresses, her love affairs, her relationship with the King – her Charles – and her relationships with his other mistresses, especially Louise de Keroualle who was a constant thorn in her side, but in typical Nell-fashion she sent up regularly in a gleefully mischievous way.

Nell has been a joy to research and write about. Her charm and wit echo down over the years and I can imagine her smart remarks, her playful nature and her light-hearted laughter. I hope I have done her justice.

Chapter One

The Early Years 1650-1662

A young woman dressed in a satin gown, her petticoats revealing a tantalising glimpse of ankle, took the stage, delivering lines that had the audience in uproar. To finish she merrily danced a jig and cocked a wink up to the royal box. The laughter of the crowd carried on after the show as the people of London spilled into the streets, finding their paths home in the dim light, smiles still on their lips. The King sent a messenger backstage to the pretty, witty actress. He requested her company for the evening, an evening that involved wine, women and song and inevitably a tussle under some silken sheets. Although they did not yet know it, their relationship would last a lifetime and be the talk of the town long after they had both gone.

Nell's early life is shrouded in mystery and plenty of colourful stories but no definite answers. As she rose in her theatrical career and found the love of a king, she may well have wanted to gloss over the truth of her childhood days. In contrast, Nell's later life is well documented as are the lives of the women who became Charles II's mistresses, but no one seems to have any proof or evidence of her early years and Nell quite possibly liked it that way – a sense of the enigmatic adding to her allure.

Nell, the pretty, witty actress who would become Charles II's favourite mistress, was born into a country that had been torn apart by war. The English Civil War began in 1642 and would continue for nine years, causing chaos and devastation until its dreadful conclusion. The reigning monarch and the succeeding king's father, Charles I, was pursued, imprisoned and ultimately executed. His family was split apart. The Queen, Henrietta Maria, would escape to France, the land of her birth, where their youngest daughter, Henrietta Anne, would join her. Their eldest daughter, Mary, married into Holland and safety whilst their middle daughter, Elizabeth, would sadly die in captivity. The Stuart sons, Charles, James and Henry, would finally make their way to the Continent

1

leaving behind a country divided in its loyalties. Ordinary people were affected the most. Fathers, brothers, uncles and sons found themselves fighting on opposite sides – for the Royalists or the Parliamentarians. Lives were lost and families torn apart. The war and the following Interregnum would cast a pall over England and blanket it in a sombre mood.

Nell could have been born in Oxford, London or Hereford. She never told anybody where, perhaps she didn't know or more likely didn't care. London became her home and that was all that mattered. But all three of these cities have a possible connection. The first suggested birthplace is Oxford. An anonymous poem written in 1681, often attributed to John Wilmot, the 2nd Earl of Rochester, who would become Nell's lifelong friend and be party to her secrets, mentions Nell and her father:

> From Oxford prison many did she free
> There dy'd her father, and there glory'd she[1]

So who was Nell's father? By the time her life was in the public eye, he was long dead and there are few mentions of him. It begs the question whether Nell actually met her father or knew who he was. Frederick Van Bossen, writing in 1688, gives us the possibility of one Thomas Gwine, a captain of an ancient family from Wales. Gwyn meaning 'fair' or 'white' is a known Welsh name. Nell's coat of arms, a blue lion on a gold and silver shield, would later be based on the Gwyns of Llansanor, Glamorgan, but any actual connection to them has not been proved.

As mentioned in the poem, her father apparently died there in gaol and another satire alludes to Nell being born in a garrison town 'for a battalion of arm'd men begot her.'[2] Frederick John Varley extensively researched the history of city of Oxford during the English Civil War. Charles I made it his Royalist base from 1642, holding court at Christ Church College while the Queen was housed at Merton College. With the siege of Oxford in 1646, it fell back under Parliamentary control. Varley compiled a list of Royalist captains stationed at the garrison town and there is no Thomas Gwyn, but there is a Rowland. He died on 19 November 1643 and was buried in the church of St Peter-le-Bailey, close to the prison also mentioned in Wood's *Ancient and Present State of the City of Oxford*. If there was a Captain Thomas there is no record of him, but he may have just been a soldier as so many of the Royalist army go unnamed and unlisted.

The soldiers that were stationed at Oxford attracted female camp followers. Some of these were women who refused to leave their husbands and followed the army and their men; others had partners they accompanied and yet more were prostitutes. It was a life not without risk. At Naseby, one hundred women followers were slaughtered and even more were mutilated, receiving heinous punishments such as nose slitting. Nell's mother may well have been one of the camp followers who travelled to Oxford from London and where she subsequently gave birth to Nell and her sister, Rose.

The antiquary Anthony Wood sketched a family tree for Nell in the back of his almanac for the year 1681. He named Nell's grandfather as Dr Edward Gwyn, canon of the fourth stall in Christ Church College, Oxford. He thought he had two sons – one unnamed (Nell's father) married a Smith (Nell's mother) of the parish of St Thomas in central-west Oxford. There was also an Uncle Henry. As Dr Edward Gwyn taught at Christ Church he would not have been able to marry, so his sons would have been illegitimate.

Charles Kirkpatrick Sharpe, an antiquarian, noted, 'When I first went to Oxford, Dr John Ireland, an antiquary, assured me that Nelly was born in Oxford. He named the parish, but I have forgot it. It is certain that two of her sons' titles – Headington and Burford – were taken from Oxford localities.'[3] In 1676 Nell's son would receive the titles of Earl of Burford and Baron of Heddington, which some have seen as establishing a family link to Oxford, but Nell would also spend many happy years here later in life. The link regarding titles is tenuous although there is more evidence of Oxford being her place of birth than London or Hereford.

Given that the surname Gwyn and its variants are Welsh it is no surprise that Nell's birthplace could also have been Hereford, sixteen miles east from the Welsh border and situated on the picturesque River Wye. One story tells us that her father left the army for Hereford after its surrender in 1646, another that her father was a smith and after he died she was cared for by her grandfather at Dinedor, a few miles south-east of Hereford. She is reputed to have been born in Pipewell Lane, later named Gwynne Street, in 1855. The actor David Garrick, writing in 1856, said, 'a building at the rear of the Royal Oak Inn is usually pointed out as the place.'[4] The old timber structured cottage that had been built on church grounds was demolished in 1859 to enlarge the gardens of the Bishop's Palace and no records survive of its occupants.

It was said that Nell asked Charles to pay for the restoration of the organ at Hereford Cathedral in honour of her birthplace, but the new organ that was built by Renatus Harris was completed in 1686 – a year after Charles II's death. The subscribers to the fund for the organ, which cost £515, are well documented in the 'Catalogue of All Benefactors of the Great Organ 1686' and the King was not one of them.

Much has been made of the fact that Nell's grandson, James Beauclerk, later served as Bishop of Hereford from 1746-1787. This is undeniable and gives us again a link, but no proof that it was his grandmother's birthplace. It seems he neither admitted nor denied the possibility. He had in fact applied for bishoprics elsewhere so was it just circumstance rather than family connection that led him there?

In an age of restricted social mobility, it would be hard to place Nell's mother in Hereford. Oxford was not far from London and from what we know about her she would have seen an opportunity there, but to travel so far was a great remove. Admittedly, she could have married a Gwyn and moved there, but there are no marriage records or any other evidence to place her close to the Welsh border. The stories of Nell's birth in Hereford are not contemporary and the earliest I have found is from 1796. It may be that the tenure of her grandson sparked the need for a connection to be made.

Although Nell's mother became more well-known as her daughter rose to fame there is also some ambiguity surrounding the details of her own life. Her epitaph was reproduced with her age at death being either LVI or LXI – so fifty-six or sixty-one – giving us two different birth years of 1618 and 1623. There are no births extant in London for either of these years although a Helena Smith was born in Tower Hamlets in 1621 and an Ellinor Smith in 1624. Her death in 1679 is well documented but so much more is missing. She was of the parish of St Martin-in-the-Fields and her tombstone, erected by Nell, would read that she was born here.

Old Ma Gwyn – also known as Ellen, Eleanor or Helen/Helena – was attributed with the maiden name 'Smith' by Anthony Wood, who compiled Nell's family tree in his *Life and Times* but he doesn't give a first name for Nell's mother. Given that it is difficult to be exactly sure of her name, and the challenge of researching the common surname, Smith, there do not appear to be any records for a marriage. Even the surname Gwyn has many variants, including Gywnn, Gwynne, Guin and Gwin. A Thomas Gywn was married in St Martin-in-the-Fields in 1663 so there was a family of Gwyns in the parish in which she lived who may have been relations. It is also possible that Gwyn was actually her maiden name.

Through her mother, Nell did have London roots, but as for the definite assertion by Captain Alexander Smith, writing in 1715, that she was born in Coal Yard Alley off Drury Lane, there is no positive proof. Coal Yard alley, a slum area off Drury Lane (named for Sir Thomas Drury), was not far from Covent Garden but no longer exists. London, however, was where she was raised, lived and died and Londoners would claim her as their own.

So Nell's birthplace – most probably Oxford, possibly London and probably not Hereford – is still open for debate; as is her year of birth. Everyone seems to agree on the day and month – 2 February – but it is more difficult to ascertain the year and it may well be that Nell covered up the truth.

Elias Ashmole, best known for his extensive collections of books and artefacts and interest in astrology and alchemy, is thought to have compiled Nell's astrological birth chart, and calculated that she was born on 2 February 1650, the year after Charles I's execution, at 6am. The chart is preserved at the Bodleian Library in Oxford but it is not without its problems. There is no place of birth given, which would have given us a better idea of where Nell was born and is essential in compiling a true chart. Her name was added at a later date and in different handwriting. Ashmole himself makes no mention of compiling her chart in his diaries, although the chart is attributed to him and was found in his papers. It is possible that it was actually the work of his mentor, William Lilly, but regardless of who actually devised her astrological chart, many have agreed with its findings: Nell was a woman of beauty, wit and charm.

The date 1650 may have been assumed to be correct but is not substantiated. Another date suggested for her birth is 'about 1642', given in 'The Manager's Note Book' published in 1838 in *The New Monthly Magazine and Humorist*, but it gives no proof of where this date comes from, and the rest of the article is riddled with inconsistencies. Both 1642 and 1650 have become the dates that are quoted for her year of birth, and neither can be proved without a doubt, but as we will see the earlier date does have its merits.

If Nell's father was really Rowland Gwyn and he had died in 1643 then a birth date of 1650 would be impossible for her and 1642 is more likely to be correct. Her mother would have then taken her back to London and raised her in her home parish. Nell would not be the first woman to lie about her age to make herself appear younger, and given the profession she ended up in and the lifestyle she kept, it was better to maintain a youthful appeal.

Nell had an older sister, Rose, whom she grew up with and would be close to later in life. Again, we don't know where or when she was born although a date of 1648 has been suggested. She would say that her father died in service to the late king, Charles I, which is the main evidence for Nell's birthplace being Oxford – but that assumes they shared the same father. They could have been half-sisters. Rose would live a promiscuous and troubled life but Nell always supported her and their mother and they would grow up together in the streets and bawdy houses of London.

*****

Covent Garden was first mentioned in 1654 as 'the new market'. The bustling trade it would become known for had only just started in Nell's childhood. Coal Yard Alley, 'a row of miserable tenements',[5] was just north of the market and a short walk from Lincoln Inn Fields. It was situated in the parish of St Giles and although we can't be sure this was exactly the place she grew up in, it would not have been far from either the family's local church at St Martin-in-the-Fields – her place of worship – or from Drury Lane, her place of work.

The young Nell would have found life on the London streets hard. Her mother sent her and her sister out to earn their living from an early age and we have various references to Nell as selling cinders or hawking fish, oysters or vegetables to bring in some coin. It was a hand-to-mouth existence, with never any money spare for new clothes or luxuries.

A satire published in 1677 and attributed to John Lacy or John Wilmot, Earl of Rochester, both men who would feature greatly in Nell's life, said

> Whose first employment was with open throat
> To cry fresh herrings, even at ten a groat[6]

Nell was one of many youths who hawked their wares on the streets of London. Childhood was short-lived and children helped the family by making money as soon as they were able. The street hawkers had their routes, walking the streets around Covent Garden, loudly calling out to passers-by to buy their wares. Fruit and vegetables were carried in baskets or trays balanced precariously on their heads. As they sauntered along their well-trodden paths they would pass by other street vendors, from knife sharpeners to ink sellers, milk and coal vendors, chair menders and clothes sellers. Everything was for sale on the streets of the city.

The first story of any romance in her life is completely innocent. Young Dick, a linkboy who carried torches to illuminate people's way in the evenings, was so enamoured of her he told her he would love her till his dying day. Nell is supposed to have recalled:

> He, poor boy, would light me and my mother home when we had sold our oranges to our lodgings in Lewkenor's Lane, as if we had been ladies of the land ... I shall never forget when he came flushing and stammering, and drew out of his pocket a pair of worsted stockings which he had bought for my naked feet. It was bitter cold weather and I had chilblains which made me hobble about till I cried. My mother bade him put them on; and so he did, and his warm tears fell on my chilblains and he said he should be the happiest Lord on earth if the stockings did me any good.'[7]

But, as with a lot of stories about Nell, there are inconsistencies. Her mother was not an orange seller and it wouldn't be until later that Nell would become an orange girl herself at the theatre. Still, it is a pleasant tale of young love and evokes a picture of Nell's early life.

Nell and her sister sold their goods while their mother was purportedly employed in the Rose Tavern in Little Russell Street, next to what would be the new theatre in Drury Lane. The tavern was known for debauchery and violence: 'in those days a man could not go from the Rose Tavern to the Piazza once but he must venture his life twice.'[8] Madame Gwyn was dismissed due to her predilection for alcohol and the drinking of at least a bottle of brandy a day, an addiction that would last her lifetime.

The most reliable account of Nell's childhood is in a conversation recorded by Samuel Pepys, the renowned diarist, in 1667. In a quarrel with Beck Marshall, another actress, Nell said, 'I was brought up in a bawdy house to fill strong waters to the guests.'[9] A bawdy house was similar to a tavern in that it was an establishment that served drinks – the strong waters or brandy that Nell spoke of – but the owners could also supply prostitutes to their customers.

Hundreds of bawdy houses and brothels opened up the year Charles II was restored. The Parliament of 1650 had tried to cut down on prostitution with its 'Act for suppressing the abominable sins of Incest, Adultery and Fornication' but it would never die out completely. The Civil War had seen many women follow the army as prostitutes, and now without soldiers or husbands they headed back to London to find work.

Madame Ross' establishment in Lewkenor's Lane was popular and Nell's mother might have worked here or managed a bawdy house of her own. She was happy for her girls to help as it meant more coin and more brandy. An anonymous biographer thought that Madam Gwyn tried to protect Nell's innocence by making her move to the countryside to relatives in Yorkshire but that Nell had 'seen enough of life to make her fond of the town, and though she was then in the full possession of her virtue, she began to entertain some thoughts of yielding it, rather than be sent to the country to live in obscurity and contract rustic habits.'[10]

It seems unlikely that Madam Gwyn would really have wanted her daughter to leave London when she was earning a wage and contributing to the family income, but how far her girls went with bawdy-house customers we'll never know.

The writer, possibly Sir George Etherege, of 'Madame Nelly's Complaint' would think Nell served up more than just brandy, writing:

Then was by Madame Ross exposed to town,
I mean to those who will give half-a-crown.[11]

Yet, Nell would always maintain that she had never worked as a prostitute, although it was a profession on the increase in the early years of Charles II's restoration and her mother and sister were associated with it. The man who she would later be forever linked with brought to his reign a relaxed and indulgent atmosphere where the excesses of pleasure were rife, but it came after years of personal struggle.

After the death of his father, Charles I, in 1649, Charles II (then Prince of Wales) led a peripatetic life. Charles II had been crowned King of Scotland at Scone Abbey on 1 January 1651, but his restoration to the English throne at that time was uncertain. The Scottish army invaded England in a bid to restore the monarchy but were defeated at the Battle of Worcester on 3 September 1651. From then on Charles was on the run. As the story goes, he once evaded capture by hiding in an oak tree at Boscobel House with Major Carlis, and after six weeks of traipsing the country in disguise he managed to escape to Holland and his sister Mary's court. Charles then fled across Europe to France where his mother, brothers and sister were living, impoverished and homeless, waiting for the day he could return home.

That day came on 25 May 1660, when Charles answered the call of a new Parliament convened after Cromwell's death and when the Lord Protector's son Richard abdicated his position. The new king took ship from Breda, landing at Dover to a rapturous welcome. General Monck, who had aided his restoration, was the first to greet him and would be ennobled as the 1st Duke of Albemarle for his service.

On 29 May, the restored king's thirtieth birthday, Charles rode into London on horseback, alongside his two brothers, James and Henry, past General Monck and his 30,000-strong army who had gathered at Blackheath. They were greeted by the Lord Mayor of London at Deptford where Charles was offered the sword of the capital and was immediately knighted. Charles continued towards Whitehall, a journey that took him seven hours:

> surrounded by a crowd of the nobility, with great pomp and triumph and in the most stately manner ever seen, amid the acclamations and blessings of the people ... The mayor and magistrates of the city met him and tendered the customary tributes, and he passed from one end to the other of this very long city, between the foot soldiers who kept the streets open, raising his eyes to the windows looking at all, raising his hat to all and consoling all who with loud shouts and a tremendous noise acclaimed the return of this great prince so abounding in virtues and distinguished qualities of every sort.[12]

At Whitehall the King continued to greet his people and the city celebrated his arrival. The Venetian ambassador reported, 'For three days and three nights they have lighted bonfires and made merry, burning effigies of Cromwell and other rebels with much abuse. The foreign ministers have taken part in these rejoicings, and I also, in addition to the illuminations have kept before the door a fountain of wine and other liquors, according to the custom of the country, much to the delight of the people and amid acclamations.'[13] He would later be crowned at Westminster Abbey on 23 April 1661.

Nell was ten or older when the restoration began. London had grown to become the second largest city in Europe, only Paris was larger, and was relatively physically unaffected by the civil war. The old city walls had survived but were no longer able to contain the bustling town, and the environs were expanding. Not only had the poor and war-affected country people flocked to the city for new opportunities but the arrival of a new monarch meant the court was a place of employment.

Charles made Whitehall Palace his home. Once owned by Cardinal Thomas Wolsey as York Place – the home of the archbishops of York – Henry VIII had it remodelled and extended making it the largest palace in Europe at the time. Subsequent monarchs had made changes over the years until Whitehall Palace became a mismatch of architecture with around 1,500 rooms including apartments, long galleries, banqueting rooms, state rooms and miles of corridors. It had its own chapels, gardens, cockpit, tennis court and entertainment buildings, including a theatre. And through its grand entrance gates was a constant stream of people.

The King was surrounded by people who found a place of work in the sprawling palace. Grooms, pages, messengers and courtiers followed in his wake. When he dressed, his groom of the stole helped him, his master of robes adorned him with jewels, esquires of the body and the royal barber helped him wash and shave. When he ate, cupbearers, servers, waiters and carvers surrounded him. His primary officers, the Lord Chancellor, Lord Treasurer and Lord Privy Seal, vied for his attention. His friends and other courtiers were never too far away. The Merry Gang – or the Court Wits – as they were called were a group of poets, rakes, womanisers, drunkards and hellraisers who kept the King amused. Men like George Villiers, 2nd Duke of Buckingham, John Wilmot, 2nd Earl of Rochester, Sir Charles Sedley, Lord Buckhurst,

Henry Savile, Harry Killigrew and Sir Carr Scrope amongst others who would also become friends with Nell. And after Charles had dealt with the day's business, there was the Keeper of the King's Privy Closet to ensure there was some female relief escorted up the backstairs into his apartments in the evenings.

England was emerging from the stiff regime that Cromwell had instilled across the country into a new and exciting place to be, with fresh opportunities and renewed hope for the future. The King and his court were the centre of attention.

Nell was too young to catch the King's eye yet, and anyway he had the nineteen-year-old Barbara Villiers, cousin to George Villiers, the 2nd Duke of Buckingham, to warm his bed. It was even rumoured she had helped him celebrate from his very first night at Whitehall. We don't know exactly when Charles first met Barbara, an auburn-haired, blue-eyed beauty who would feature in his life for a long time to come, but one suggestion is that she was used to take messages to the exiled King in Breda. Her father was Lord Grandison – a staunch Royalist and supporter of Charles I – and she had married another Royalist, Roger Palmer, in 1659. He, too, had supported the return of the King and donated £1,000 to Charles' cause. Barbara's marriage was not a happy one. She had been the lover of the Earl of Chesterfield before she married Palmer and continued the affair long after.

Although Barbara was the King's chief mistress, he certainly had no bent towards monogamy and there would be many other women who shared his bed. It has been suggested that the boredom of exile fuelled his sexual desires and that he had nothing better to do than pass his time in the company of women. By now he had five illegitimate children and one on the way. James had been born to Lucy Walter in 1649, Charlotte to Elizabeth Killigrew in 1650, Charles and Catherine to Catherine Pegge in 1657 and 1658, and Anne (although her parentage is debated) to Barbara Villiers who was expecting their second child. It was now time to take the next step to produce a legitimate heir.

On 21 May 1662 a wedding took place in Portsmouth: two in fact, one private and one public. Catherine of Braganza, a Portuguese and Catholic princess, had made the terrible journey from her homeland, beaten back by storms on several occasions, to finally arrive on England's shores. Church bells rang out across London and bonfires were lit to celebrate the arrival of the new Queen but gossip soon spread that no fires were lit at Barbara's house. The King, who should have been on his way to meet Catherine, was instead playing with his pregnant mistress: 'the King and she did send for a pair of scales and weighed one another; and she, being with child, was said to be heaviest.'[14] If the King could not take his marriage seriously, it was not a good omen.

Catherine was the daughter of the wealthiest nobleman in Portugal, the Duke of Braganza, and had led a rather sheltered life. Nothing could have prepared her for what she was about to be hurled into. The English court was far removed from the sombreness and piety of the Portuguese court – she could never have imagined what she was about to endure. Charles wasn't bothered that he kept his wife-to-be waiting. He was having fun with Barbara – his wedding could wait. His new Queen meant little to him other than the fact that she brought to England a huge dowry in the region of £500,000 and the ports of Bombay and Tangier as well as trading rights.

On first meeting Catherine of Braganza, Charles thought:

> Her face is not so exact as to be called a beauty, though her eyes are excellent good, and nothing in her face that in the least degree can disgust one. On the contrary she has as much agreeableness in her looks as I ever saw and if I have any skill in physiognomy, which I think I have, she must be as good a woman as ever was born. Her conversation as much as I can perceive, is very good, for she has wit enough, and a most agreeable voice; in a word, I think myself very happy, for I am confident our two humours will agree very well.[15]

It would be a while before they found their balance. Catherine brought the King the potential for an heir and money for his coffers, although most of it had come in goods rather than cash, much to his dismay. Her foreignness was, however, a target for gossip and laughter. People smirked at her Portuguese hairstyle and dress. She wore old-fashioned farthingale dresses with wide-hooped skirts and her hair was an unfashionable wide mop of curls that Charles thought made her look like a bat. She was not a beauty by English standards and Barbara, who had feared the Queen would unsettle her hold over the King, saw she had nothing to worry about.

The new Queen's state entry into London followed in August. A royal aquatic progress, or *Aqua Triumphalis*, was organised instead of a coronation. Catherine and Charles travelled by river barge eight miles from Hampton Court before they swopped to a larger boat with glass windows and a red and gold canopy. At Putney, where twenty-four scarlet-clad bargemen awaited to row them into London, they embarked on the state barge decorated with the royal arms and a canopy of gold brocade. The diarist, John Evelyn wrote:

> I was spectator of the most magnificent triumph that ever floated on the Thames, considering the innumerable boats and vessels, dressed with all imaginable pomp; but, above all, the thrones, arches, pageants, and other representations, stately barges of the lord mayor and companies, with various inventions, music, and peals of ordnance, both from the vessels and the shore, going to conduct the new queen from Hampton Court to Whitehall, at the first of her coming to town. In my opinion, it far exceeded all the Venetian Bucentoras, &c, on the occasion when they go to espouse the Adriatic. His majesty and the queen came in an antique-shaped open vessel, covered with a state or canopy of cloth of gold, made in the form of a high cupola, supported with high Corinthian pillars, wreathed with flowers, festoons, and garlands.[16]

The people of the city gathered along the riverside to welcome Catherine to London. It was a fantastic excuse for days of celebration, to shake off the years of austerity and the dreadful memories of the Civil War.

Nell must have seen and heard the celebrations, jostling through the crowds to get a better look and marvelling at the opulence of the King and his new Queen. Did she yearn to be part of that world already? She had certainly noticed her sovereign. Once Charles settled into a daily routine she often used to see him striding around St James and Hyde Park with his beloved spaniels or playing tennis. The King enjoyed being in the public eye and prided himself on being accessible to his subjects.

Charles was a strapping figure with tumbling black locks, a dark complexion, handsome face and sensuous mouth. He had embraced the pleasures of life rather enthusiastically after his restoration and the

Restoration court was fast becoming a place of pleasure and scandal where the King, his courtiers and his mistress drank, gambled and whored every night, the Queen quietly keeping to her rooms.

Whether the Queen knew of Charles' illegitimate children, his string of mistresses and his current lover before she set sail from Portugal we don't know, but she quickly came up to speed regarding Barbara Villiers, who had given birth to the King's son on 18 June.

When Charles gave the Queen a list of ladies to approve for her household, she crossed out her name and refused to have the woman anywhere near her. But Charles persisted, even bringing Barbara to meet the Queen. Catherine hadn't realised who the woman was until one of her ladies whispered the truth in her ear. Salty tears welled in her eyes, blood streamed from her nose, and then she collapsed in a dead faint. It would lead to the first of many arguments between the King and Queen.

Barbara would not give up easily. Clarendon reported that she followed the Queen as if she was one of her ladies and 'she thrust herself into the royal coach, and went wherever the queen went – to the park, the theatre, to the houses of the nobility.'[17] Poor Catherine would be hounded by Barbara, the King and the Lord Chancellor, who tried to act as a mediator between an enraged King and a distressed Queen. Charles refused to back down. He wanted Barbara as one of the Queen's ladies of the bedchamber. She came from a good family and it would honour them if he gave her the position. The Queen swore she would rather return to Lisbon in disgrace than put up with the King's mistress.

For a while it was stalemate. Clarendon tried to persuade her to back down even though there was no love lost between himself and Barbara. He was the Lord Chancellor and had to do his sovereign's bidding. He told the Queen, 'it was presumed that no wife would refuse to receive a servant that was esteemed and recommended by her husband, and that it was better for her to submit in this instance than that it should be done without her consent.' Catherine told him, 'that the king might do what he pleased, but she never would consent.'[18]

Barbara was a hard woman to come up against. She had the King's favour, her own supporters at court and she was mother to his children, all of which Catherine struggled with, as an outsider. Her main aim, and what was expected of her, was to provide Charles with an heir but it would prove impossible. While she became pregnant on several occasions, she would never give the King any children. The years of trying were yet to come but for now there was the problem of the King's mistress. Surprisingly, Catherine was about to give in.

Charles' eldest son by Lucy Walters, James, who had adopted the surname Crofts, had recently arrived at court. Later to be given the title Duke of Monmouth, he would become a firm friend of Nell's and was popular with all the ladies and the King's mistresses. Pepys was a fly on the wall at Somerset House when he saw Barbara and Monmouth together: 'Here I also saw Madam Castlemaine, and, which pleased me most, Mr. Crofts, the King's bastard, a most pretty spark of about 15 years old, who, I perceive, do hang much upon my Lady Castlemaine, and is always with her; and, I hear, the Queens both of them are mighty kind to him. By and by in comes the King, and anon the Duke and his Duchess; so that, they being all together, was such a sight as I never could almost have happened to see with so much ease and leisure.'[19]

Something happened to make the Queen give in. It might have been meeting the King's eldest child and watching his mistress flirt with him. They were both so accepted at court that Catherine realised she would have to learn to live with all of the King's children and his mistresses. So she relented, but even that did not make her any friends. Clarendon wrote: 'This total abandoning her own greatness, this lowly demeanour to a person she had justly contemned, made all men conclude that it was a hard matter to know her, and consequently to serve her. And the king himself was so far from being reconciled by it, that the esteem which he could not hitherto in his heart but retain for her, grew now much less. He concluded that all her former anguish, expressed in those lively passions which seemed not capable of dissimulation, was all fiction, and purely acted to the life by a nature crafty, perverse, and inconstant.'[20]

Charles was not quite the 'merry monarch' in the early years of his marriage – not with the Queen anyway. In time, though, they would find a balance and eventually come to care for one another. The King was a man of excess but he was also an astute and shrewd ruler. He was interested in the creative arts, literature and science, patronising the Royal Society of London for Improving Natural Knowledge, an early organisation for the promotion and exploration of science. He was a complex man – not just all about pleasure – but much more.

Later in 1750, one of his chief ministers, George Savile, the Marquis of Halifax, wrote with mixed feelings of his capabilities: 'He had a mechanical head, which appeared in his inclination to shipping and fortification, &c. This would make one conclude, that his thoughts would naturally have been more fixed to business, if his pleasures had not drawn them away from it. He had a very good memory, though he would not always make equal good use of it. So that if he had accustomed himself to direct his faculties to his business, I see no reason why he might not have been a good deal master of it.'

Halifax admitted that as the King grew older he found a balance: 'He grew by age into a pretty exact distribution of his hours, both for his business, pleasures, and the exercise for his health, of which he took as much care as could possibly consist with some liberties he was resolved to indulge in himself. He walked by his watch, and when he pulled it out to look upon it, skilful men would make hast with what they had to say to him.'[21]

Gilbert Burnet in his *A History of His Own Time* also had mixed feelings about the King. It seems that Charles' personality was hard to pin down, it made people wonder how many facets he truly had, and writers found it difficult to define him. Burnet thought he had a good understanding of state affairs but hated business. He had a great compass of knowledge but wasn't capable of application or study. Charles, he wrote, was affable and easy. But perhaps that is exactly what he wanted people to believe and underneath it all was a perceptive and astute ruler.

One of his foremost acts was to sign a fundamental patent – a momentous occasion in the history of theatre and something that would change the course of Nell's life – one that would allow women on the stage for the first time.

> And for as much as many plays formerly acted do contain several profane, obscene and scurrilous passages, and the women's parts therein have been acted by men in the habit of women, at which some have taken offence, for the preventing of these abuses in the future, we do hereby strictly command and enjoin that from henceforth … we do likewise permit and give leave that all women's parts to be acted in either of the said two companies for the time to come, may be performed by women so long as these recreations, which, by reasons of the abuses aforesaid were scandalous and offensive, may by such reformation be esteemed not only

harmless delights but useful and instructive representations
of human life to such of our good subjects as shall resort to
the same.[22]

This was a huge step. Not only was the King reducing something
heretofore seen as scandalous and offensive to a harmless delight – which
could sum up his reign – he was giving women a professional freedom
they had never had before. It opened up a new career path for daughters
of shopkeepers, preachers, notaries and down-on-their-luck gentlemen –
women we shall meet in a later chapter – women who would otherwise
have had to go into service or seek a husband for security. Experienced
actresses could expect 30s a week, less experienced ones 10-15s. Acting,
though, wasn't the realm of 'ladies' and the profession would be frowned
upon by some, likening those first actresses to whores, but the women
who took to the stage in the Restoration period were making history.

Some women had graced the stage before. French troupes visiting
London would have had female roles and, of course, in court plays ladies
often amused themselves by taking part at royal spectacles, but this was
the first time that true actresses were seen. It is up for debate who had
the honour of being the very first who took to the stage. It could have
been Anne Marshall or Mary Saunderson, perhaps Katherine Corey or
Mrs Norton, but what is known is the role they played was Desdemona
in *Othello,* a Shakespearean classic.

Whilst the actual legal position of women did not change, Charles'
reign ushered in a more relaxed and lenient atmosphere. Lorenzo
Magalotti, an Italian diplomat, described the women of London in his
journal:

> The women of London are not inferior to the men either in
> stature or in beauty, for they are all of them handsome, and
> for the most part tall, with black eyes, abundance of light-
> coloured hair, and a neatness which is extreme ... They live
> with all the liberty that the custom of the country authorises.
> This custom dispenses with that rigorous constraint and
> reservedness which are practised by the women of other
> countries, and they go whithersoever they please, either
> alone or in company; and those of the lower order frequently
> go as far as to lay at ball publicly in the streets ... they do

not easily fall in love, nor throw themselves into the arms of men, but if they are smitten by the amorous passion they become infatuated and sacrifice all their substance for the sake of the beloved object, and if he deserts them, they are sunk into great despair and affliction. Their style of dressing is very elegant, entirely after the French fashion, and they take more pride in rich clothes (which are worn of value even by women of the lowest rank) than in rich jewels ... Such and so great is the respect which the English entertain for their women that in their houses, the latter govern everything despotically, making themselves feared by the men.[23]

And Nell would in time sacrifice all her substance for the love of the King. For now, she still had some growing up to do on the hard streets of London. Nell's education was the school of life. She didn't have any type of formal education and was known to be illiterate – only able to sign her name with 'E.G.', which makes her all the more remarkable as an actress. She was about to take a step toward her new career.

Chapter Two

On the Stage 1663-1665

Nell moved out of the slum dwellings that she shared with her mother and Rose to the Cock & Pie, a tavern frequented by actors at the top of Maypole Alley, not far from where Thomas Killigrew was building his new theatre. A later print shows the inn's sign of a cockerel and a magpie, but it is thought the name originally came from 'Peacock in a Pie' referring to a medieval dish. However, Drury Lane was also a cock-fighting area and it may be a nod to that. This print interestingly also shows a street girl touting for work by the side of the tavern and a man recoiling in horror (see illustration No.11).

An apocryphal story tells us that Nell was so upset at the King's marriage to Catherine of Braganza that she took up with a merchant (or an officer in the guards – stories differ), Robert Duncan (or Dongan/ Dungan) who 'taking a fancy to her smart wit, fine shape and foot, the least of any woman's in England, kept her about two years and then recommended her into the king's Playhouse, where she became an actress in great vogue.'[1] Duncan was known to frequent Madame Ross' bawdy house and they may have met while Nell was serving there. It is unlikely that he introduced her to the actors of the King's Playhouse, as she already had connections to the theatrical crowd through her mother and her work as a serving girl, but Duncan did pay for their lodgings at the Cock & Pie and bought her clothes and gifts. Nell was a kept woman but little is known of her first love.

Love or necessity? An early biographer suggested, 'She now had observed how gaily many ladies lived who had no other means of supporting their grandeur but by making such concessions to men of fortune, and stipulating such terms as both of them could afford to comply with.'[2] These were times when keeping a mistress was not only normal, but, especially for men with stable incomes, deemed appropriate and necessary for their social standing. Francis North, Lord Guildford, for one, was scorned among his friends for not keeping a whore as they felt it would be 'ill looked upon at Court.'[3]

Here is another hint though that Nell could have been older than her 1650 birth date supposes. If she was living with Duncan in early 1663, she would have only been twelve, nearly thirteen – not improbable – but more likely she was older. When it came to marriage the age of consent was generally sixteen for a boy and fourteen for a girl, though marriage was far from Nell's mind. She could not have been described as a 'woman' at this tender age as mentioned above, but if she was actually born in 1642 she would have been a budding young woman nearing her twenty-first birthday.

Her relationship with the man would not last long. As the satire *The Lady of Pleasure,* sometimes attributed to Sir George Etherege, put it: 'For either with expence of purse or prick /At length the weary fool grew Nelly-sick.'[4] Another profane poem attributed Duncan's later military career to Nell: 'Duncan, by my great sway and power preferred/ For mounting me well first, now mounts the guard.'[5] It seems that Nell brought out the bawdy in everyone!

Cunningham, in his early biography of Nell, tried to find out more about Duncan and believed that he had mistakenly been identified as a merchant. He found evidence of a Robert Dongan referred to in the poem above who became a lieutenant in the Duke of York's Life Guards. Whoever he was, he gave Nell a start, a helping hand and raised her out of the slums into a much more comfortable way of living. Yet, by the summer of 1663 Nell and Duncan parted ways and she moved into rooms at the Cat & Fiddle tavern on Lewkenor's Lane, not far from Madame Ross' bawdy house. Lewkenor's Lane was named after Sir Lewes Lewkenor who had served James I as Master of Ceremonies and the street off Drury Lane was well known as 'a rendezvous and nursery for lewd women.'[6]

The theatre and the joy of watching a play had been suppressed in Cromwell's times, after the English Civil War and the execution of Charles I. The Puritan regime despised the frivolity of such entertainment, feeling that the theatre promoted debauchery and a lack of morality. William Prynne felt 'it hath evermore been the notorious badge of prostituted strumpets and the lewdest Harlots to ramble abroad to plays and to Playhouses wither only branded whores and infamous adulteresses did usually resort.'[7] On 6 September 1642 plays were banned by the Long Parliament, which would control the country until the monarchy's restoration. Stage plays were deemed 'lascivious merth and levity' and not an acceptable form of entertainment. Five years later, the destruction of stage galleries, seats and boxes was ordered and actors were to be whipped or worse – even having their tongue 'bored through with a red hot iron.'[8] Those that were found watching plays were to be fined five shillings.

On 11 February 1648 Parliament enshrined this belief in law and made actors liable to punishment, but plays went on even though the performers were arrested and theatres raided. There was no stopping the people's love of drama, nor the actors who continued to stage plays even though they were at risk of punishment.

Many flocked to Charles' court abroad and performed before the King prior to his return to England. Charles' love of theatre was in direct contrast to the strict rules imposed on England during the Interregnum. After the country was torn apart by civil war and oppressed by Cromwell's New Model Army, it now swung completely the other way. Charles was a king who loved his pleasures, and embraced the good things in life to the extreme, so it was no surprise that on his return 'the city erupted into one giant party which was to last the rest of his life.'[9] Restoring the theatres was high on his list.

Nell would embody the spirit of Restoration England as one of the first generation of female actresses, becoming famous for her comic performances. Some joked that the reason women were now allowed to appear on stage was because Edward Kynaston, one of the top actors of the time who played women's roles, and was 'a Compleat Female Stage Beauty, performing his parts so well',[10] took too long to shave his beard!

Charles II granted licences for two theatre companies: Thomas Killigrew for the King's Company and William Davenant for the Duke's Company. Davenant prepared a draft for the King to sign that read: 'Our will and pleasure is that you prepare a Bill for our signature to passe our Greate Seale of England, containing a Grant unto our trusty and well beloved Thomas Killigrew Esquire, one of the Groomes of our Bed-chamber and Sir William Davenant Knight, to give them full power and authoritie to erect Two Companys of Players consisting respectively of such persons as they shall chuse and appoint; and to purchase or build and erect at their charge as they shall thinke fit Two Houses or Theaters.'[11]

Killigrew's father had been a member of James I's court and his son became page of honour to the King's son. Thomas loved theatre from an early age and as a teenager volunteered to be a devil on stage at the Red Bull tavern. He had been writing plays well before the English Civil War. Once war broke out, Killigrew was on the Royalist side and followed his prince into exile in 1647, serving him in countries across Europe. He continued writing plays although they were not performed.

Killigrew returned to England on the *Royal Charles* in 1660 with his now King. Pepys saw him aboard, 'Walking upon the decks, where persons of honour all the afternoon, among others, Thomas Killigrew (a merry droll, but a gentleman of great esteem with the King), who told us many merry stories.'[12] He was made a Groom of the Bedchamber and Chamberlain to Queen Catherine. His wit and smart comments kept him high in the King's favour. Pepys noted that Killigrew had the office of the King's fool and jester and that he got away with mocking everyone without penalty: 'Tom Killigrew hath a fee out of the wardrobe for cap and bells, under the title of the King's foole or Jester, and may with privilege revile or jeer anybody, the greatest person, without offence, by the privilege of his place.'[13]

Davenant was a few years older than Killigrew and he too had written tragedies and tragicomedies before the war. He came under the patronage of Queen Henrietta Maria, Charles' mother, and was appointed as poet laureate in 1638, after the death of Ben Jonson. He had hoped to build a theatre then but the civil uprising thwarted his plans. Instead, he supported the prince in exile by running supplies across the English Channel and was knighted for his valiant efforts in 1643. He joined his king-to-be in Paris until he was sent to America as lieutenant governor of Maryland. However, he was captured aboard ship and sent to the Tower of London until 1654.

Nell would come to know both of these colourful men well, but the King's Company would become her own. Their first venue was at Gibbon's Tennis Court on Vere Street – a sparse building with hard wooden benches, poorly lit and freezing cold with a lack of scenery and machines. So it was not long before a better theatre was needed to keep up with their rivals.

The King's Playhouse theatre would cost around £2,500 to build, £1,000 more than estimated. Killigrew rented the site of a riding school between Bridges Street and Drury Lane for £50 a year and built his new wooden theatre on the site of today's Theatre Royal, Drury Lane. It had three tiers: the cheapest seats were the benches in the pit; boxes were more expensive; and there were two galleries. The upper gallery was reserved for footmen and servants who were allowed in at no cost during the last act. The King, of course, had his own royal box and many a play succeeded because of his enthusiastic reaction.

Whereas the tennis court had been open to the elements, the new playhouse was enclosed and had more space. The stage was covered by a tiled roof and a glass cupola was erected over the pit to let in more light, but unfortunately it still leaked, to the point that at one performance Pepys and his wife were caught in a hailstorm and had to flee to a nearby inn. Under the stage there was space for an orchestra and dressing rooms. The main actors had their own rooms with a mirror, chairs, a table and a chamber pot, while the others had 'the women's shift' and 'the men's shift' to get ready for their performances. There was a scene room for the storage of props too. Davenant had already utilised scenery and 'machines' in his theatre at Lincoln Inn's Fields and Killigrew would now follow suit in a bid to keep up with the competition.

As, for the time being, no new plays were available, both companies were allowed their allocation of pre-1660 plays to perform throughout the September to June season. Killigrew was allowed *Othello*, *The Merry Wives of Windsor* and *A Midsummer's Night's Dream* while Davenant grabbed *Romeo and Juliet*, *Macbeth* and *Twelfth Night* to name a few. Men like Dryden, Wycherley, Otway and Etherege would soon produce new plays, but for now audiences were content to see their old favourites return to the stage. Imagine the joy of the public as finally one of the most popular forms of entertainment returned to London. There would be crowds waiting for the doors to open at noon and people would happily wait up to three hours for the afternoon performance, which usually started around 3pm and lasted for another three hours.

The King's Playhouse was open to the public on 7 May 1663. The first performance in the new theatre was of *The Humorous Lieutenant,* a tragicomedy written by John Fletcher that ran for twelve nights. Samuel Pepys, the infamous diarist of this period, went on the second night of the new theatre opening, being too busy the day before, and had mixed feelings:

> The house is made with extraordinary good contrivance, and yet hath some faults, as the narrowness of the passages in and out of the Pitt, and the distance from the stage to

the boxes, which I am confident cannot hear; but for all other things it is well, only, above all, the musique being below, and most of it sounding under the very stage, there is no hearing of the bases at all, nor very well of the trebles, which sure must be mended.

The play was "The Humerous Lieutenant," a play that hath little good in it, nor much in the very part which, by the King's command, Lacy now acts instead of Clun. In the dance, the tall devil's actions was very pretty.[14]

The theatre attracted people from all walks of life, rich and poor alike. Mary Meggs, known as 'Orange Moll', was a former prostitute who lived in St Paul's, Covent Garden. Known as a local gossip, she knew all the latest scandals and passed them on to Pepys. She was given a licence 'with full, free and sole liberty, license, power and authority to vend, utter and sell oranges, lemons, fruit, sweetmeats and all manner of fruiterers and confectioners wares,'[15] and to store her goods in a room at the theatre. This was the playhouse's refreshment for its audience, offered at breaks with cries of 'Oranges! Will you have any oranges?' Meggs was also an old friend of Nell's mother, Madam Gwyn, and when she was looking for three girls to help her, she picked Nell and her sister, Rose. Both of the girls had learned how to deal with rowdy customers, and their pretty faces, slender figures and smart tongues made them an obvious choice. 'A Panegyric upon Nelly' (see Appendix II) later described Nell as an orange girl:

> But first the Basket her fair arm did suit.
> Laden with Pippins and Hesperian Fruit.
> This first step rais'd, to the wond'ring Pit she sold,
> The lovely Fruit, smiling with streaks of Gold.[16]

The girls were to work six days a week with a day off on Sunday, and were dressed in white smocks with a handkerchief tied jauntily around their necks. They sold the sweet oranges for sixpence – the oranges were originally from China but some sellers grew their own and they were also cultivated in St James Park physic garden. Pepys was even tempted to try them juiced: 'Here, which I never did before, I drank a glass, of a pint, I believe, at one draught, of the juice of oranges, of whose peel they make comfits; and here they drink the juice as wine, with sugar, and it is very fine drink; but, it being new, I was doubtful whether it might not do me hurt.'[17]

The girls stood with their backs to the stage, waiting in the pits for their cue to stroll amongst the audience selling their wares. Oranges were never sold to the upper galleries from where they could turn into deadly missiles if the audience took offence at a play. Nell may have started her life in the theatre selling the sweet fruit but she also ran messages between gentlemen and ladies, actors and their admirers. Extra tips could be gleaned for running errands. Orange girls, or 'wenches', were known for their cheeky banter and beguiling, powerful voices. Their role at the theatre has been likened to an informal sideshow and a part of the performance, as much a part of the theatre experience as the actors. The audience expected to hear their playful cries, buy their wares and set up assignations through them with a few coins. And their notoriety for profanity was infamous. The Duchess of Portsmouth would later say of Nell that you could tell she had been an orange girl by her swearing.

Orange girls were also known to work as prostitutes. That doesn't mean that Nell or Rose were working girls at this time, but prostitution was rife at the theatre where clandestine meetings could be so easily arranged. The taverns around Drury Lane and Covent Garden were a favourite haunt for paid encounters of a clandestine nature, as were the dark alleys close to the theatre. It was a place for the 'harlots, whores, lewd women and vagrant nightwalkers of London'[18] to find customers, and for clients to purchase their wares.

In fact, prostitution had risen to new heights. It was estimated that one in ten women worked the streets but that does not include the women who worked in bawdy houses and other establishments. Years of civil unrest and the loss of a stable way of life saw an influx of women to a city that had few employment opportunities. Many women turned to earning a wage with their bodies due to poverty and many did so unwillingly. It was a risky profession where the women often encountered violent clients, 'women of this class, whose voices were unheard and who were virtually sidelined by society and the law, had little recourse in the tragedies that befell them.'[19] A locksmith from Nantwich thought he had the answer to prostitution and suggested that all unmarried girls from twelve years of age up should be padlocked until they wed. He would even make the padlocks himself! So many of these women had been married and had once had stable family lives but were forced to find work – in whatever way they could – after losing their husbands in the war.

Becoming a favoured mistress, as Nell would do, meant a steadier income and more security for women, with even the chance of marriage. And there were plenty of rich men at the theatre. Evelyn unhappily wrote: 'Women now (& never 'til now) permitted to appear & act, which inflaming several young noble-men and gallants, became their whores, & to some their wives, witness the Earl of Oxford, Sir Robert Howard, Prince Rupert, the Earl of Dorset, & another greater person than any of these, who fell into their snares, to the reproach of their noble families, & ruin both of body and soul.'[20]

It meant more protection but only for as long as the relationship lasted, and this type of liaison could be fleeting, especially as a woman aged and there were prettier, younger girls eager to take her place. The wisest of mistresses put aside money, jewellery or goods to have something to fall back on. Being a cast-off mistress was not a happy prospect.

It wasn't just the women who were known for sexual promiscuity though. The actors too had a name for themselves, summed up in Robert Gould's description:

> A pack of idle, pimping, spunging slaves,
> A miscellaney of Rogues, fools & knaves,
> A nest of leachers worse than Sodom bore,
> And justly merit to be punisht more.
> Diseas'd, in debt, & every moment dun'd,
> By all good Xtians loath'd & their own kindred shun'd.[21]

London was embracing its freedom and licentiousness. The King was setting his own example. Charles had a personal pimp, William Chiffinch, Keeper of the King's Closet and Pictures, who found willing girls for him to bed. Many came from brothels and playhouses, including Elizabeth Farley and Beck Marshall. Apart from Charles, Chiffinch was the only one to have a key to the King's closet – not even the Queen could enter his private place without permission. Nor would she have wanted to, in fear of what she might find.

When she had time off, Nell enjoyed the sights and sounds of London. She remained friends with John Pritchard, the son of the owner of the Cock & Pie, who went with her to cockfights. Even though she was earning very little at this point, she loved to bet on the outcome. And there was so much more to see: bear baiting, wrestling, fencing matches, puppet shows, ballad singers, prize-fighting. She could take a stroll through the parks and pleasure gardens around the city or take a trip to the royal menagerie at the Tower of London. The supper parties that her friends at the theatre gave were a popular way to spend an evening. For the more morbidly curious, the inmates of Bedlam held a strange fascination and then there was the festival-like atmosphere of a public execution which Nell was said to enjoy.

While Nell was enjoying life, her sister had managed to get herself in trouble. Rose married John Cassells, a soldier in the Duke of Monmouth's guards, who told her that his father once had a considerable estate in Ireland but had lost it all. He would rise to captain but also quite possibly supplemented his income from highway robbery. Whether he was a bad influence or not, Rose was arrested for burglary and sent to Newgate gaol in December 1663.

But Rose had friends in high places, two of whom had visited her in prison. She wrote to Harry Browne: 'Thanks for his and Mr. Killigrew's civil visit. Begs them to obtain her release on bail from this woeful place of torment, till a pardon is pleaded. Her father lost all he had in service of the late King, and it is hard she should perish in a gaol. Was never a thief, and was pardoned before judgment, but none know when the pardon will be pleaded.'[22]

The Killigrew she refers to was the theatre manager's son, Harry (or Henry), one of Charles II's friends. His mother was Cecilia Crofts, who had been a maid of honour to the King's mother, Queen Henrietta Maria, and his father's first wife. It is not known how Rose knew Harry Browne, the Duke of York's cupbearer, unless it was also through the theatre, although some have suggested they both could have been her clients. The letter proves that the court, Charles' friends, and, by extension, the King himself, were not so far removed from the lives of the Gwyn sisters.

Rose's appeal worked. Four days later a warrant was given to a messenger, John Wickham, from the King to discharge her. 'Whereas we are given that Rose Gwynne, having been convicted of [...] at the late sessions held at the Old Bailey, was yet reprieved by the bench before judgment, and reserved as an object of our princely compassion and mercy, upon humble suite made to us in favour of the said Rose, we have thought good hereby to signify our Royal pleasure unto you, that you forthwith grant her liberty and grant discharge upon good bail first taken in order to the sueing out her pardon, and rendering our gracious mercy and compassion to be effectual.'[23]

Rose had had a lucky break, and given her connections it is quite possible that Nell had already met the King by now. The man who would soon encompass Nell's life was still married to a woman he loved but didn't lust after and barely slept with. The woman who ruled his libido was his chief mistress, Barbara, and she made sure everyone knew it. On 23 February 1663 Pepys noted that she was more bejewelled than the Queen or the Duchess of York. Many mistresses flaunted their position and outshone their lover's spouses but Barbara would always go one step more.

Yet there were many others who caught the King's eye. He could never be faithful to any one woman. In 1664 Charles was caught up in his admiration for Frances Stuart who had returned from his mother's court in France to become one of the Queen's maids of honour. She was the daughter of Walter Stuart, one of Queen Henrietta Maria's physicians at the court in Paris where Frances was born on 8 July 1647. She was famed for her beauty – Pepys practically swooned over her and she had many admirers, from the Duke of Buckingham to Francis Digby, son of the Earl of Bristol, but it was said of her that 'it would be difficult to imagine less brain combined with more beauty.'[24] Her favourite pastime was building castles from playing cards! The members of the Merry Gang thought she would be a perfect distraction for Charles, nothing as demanding as Barbara, and convened a 'Committee for the Getting of Mistress Stuart for the King'.

Frances had initially got on well with Barbara and had been taken her under her wing. Pepys had heard a delicious rumour that the King's mistress had put on a mock marriage with Frances – 'at night began a frolique that they two must be married, and married they were, with ring and all other ceremonies of church service, and ribbands and a sack posset in bed, and flinging the stocking'[25] – which the King was most delighted with. But Barbara's plan to use her for the King's amusement for one just night backfired and Charles became more and more infatuated with her.

It had gone so far that his affection for the young girl had progressed 'to the open slighting of the Queene ...he values not who sees him or stands by him while he dallies with her openly; and then privately in her chamber below, where the very sentrys observe his going in and out.'[26]

Frances was playing a dangerous game by keeping the King at arm's length. He was not a man to wait for something he wanted, but she had no intention of becoming his mistress and valued her morality. She did enjoy the attention and shared stolen kisses with the amorous sovereign but nothing more. Barbara had favoured Frances and encouraged the King's relationship with her, but now it drove her to distraction as she felt her control slipping away. Charles too was driven crazy by his desire for Frances and angrily said that one day he would see her 'ugly and willing.'[27] Nell was far away from the intrigues at court – for the moment – but it would not be long before she would give the King what Frances never would.

Amorous liaisons to one side there was more serious news that would affect the whole country that spring. On 4 March 1665 the King officially declared war on the Netherlands. To announce it to the public, heralds paraded through the streets of London pinning up notices on doors. It was the first time that Anglo-Dutch relationships had broken down since the Interregnum. Many of the male actors signed up to fight, giving female actresses even more opportunities to be on the stage.

Nell was either a teenager or in her early twenties when Charles Hart and John Lacy of the King's Company began training her for her new career. She had watched as the company's actresses – Katherine Corey, Anne Marshall, Mary Knepp – had delivered their lines and she had seen how they were treated. They were fawned over, adored, given gifts and wore sumptuous clothes. They also earned anything from twenty to fifty shillings a week and that was something Nell could aspire to.

Lacy was a leading comedian, playwright and choreographer. He was one of the King's favourites but would get into trouble for delivering subversive lines in 1667. He had at one time been a dancing master and now he was teaching Nell how to dance the jigs she would become famous for. He was nearing fifty but still it was rumoured that they were having an affair. Colley Cibber, an actor, playwright and theatre manager himself would later write, 'Hart introduced Mrs. Gwyn upon the dramatic boards, and has acquired the distinction of being ranked among that lady's first felicitous lovers, by having succeeded to Lacy in the possession of her charms.'[28] Sir George Etherege also thought Nell, the 'harlot of harlots'[29] had been with Lacy and moved on to Hart.

Charles Hart was approximately ten years younger than Lacy. It was once believed he was the grandson of Shakespeare's sister, Joan Hart, but that has since been disproved. He fought in the civil war under Prince Rupert of the Rhine but escaped to the continent with other English actors, performing in The Hague and before Prince Charles in Paris. Hart, along with Lacy and Michael Mohun, an actor in Queen Henrietta's Men in the reign of Charles I, became a co-manager of the King's Company. Hart had shares in the company and helped other actors with their finances and debts. He was one of its leading actors, playing roles such as Amintor in *The Maid's Tragedy*, Rollo in *The Bloody Brother*, and Michael Perez in *Rule a Wife and Have a Wife,* as well as female parts. Now he would help to coach Nell and go on to co-star alongside her as well as being her lover.

The satirist Tom Browne wrote, 'Tis as hard a matter for a pretty Woman to keep herself honest in a Theatre, as tis for an Apothecary to keep his Treacle from the Flies in Hot Weather; for every Libertine in the Audience will be buzzing about her Honeypot, and her Virtue must defend itself by abundance of fly-flaps, or those Flesh-loving Insects will soon blow upon her Honour, and when once she has a Maggot in her Tail, all the Pepper and Salt in the Kingdom will scarce keep her Reputation from Stinking.'[30] But Nell's reputation would not suffer from their relationship. Instead, it would thrive and they would become the power couple of the theatrical world. But for now Nell had to learn more than just the plays. She had to learn how to deliver different types of roles and how to act in a physical setting. Rehearsals took place in the morning and for established actors who spent the evenings at parties and rowdy taverns that was a hard call that could cost them a week's wages if they didn't show.

Killigrew thought she was progressing well. In a play he was writing at the time, *Thomaso, or The Wanderer*, which, as far as we know, was never performed, he noted 'Nelly' against the part of 'Paulina, a courtesan of the first rank.'[31] It's also possible that she had a bit part in Sir William Killigrew's *The Siege of Urbin*, performed in 1664-65. Anne Marshall was the lead actress but 'Mrs Nell' was written next to Pedro/ Malina – a 'breeches' role. Breeches roles were male parts played by female actresses and their trousers were figure-hugging and typically ended at the knee. Women had never dressed this way before and for the audience it was extremely revealing and erotic. Nell became known for her fine legs, which were shown off to great effect by wearing men's clothes. There were specific instructions for the ladies, 'Florio (Anne) and Pedro (Nell) must not fight on the stage through the whole play.'[32] Apparently, they either couldn't be trusted to fight nicely or were unable to handle their swords!

Nell's date of birth can be questioned here as well. If the Mrs Nell was our Nell then that was a term more commonly used for older women not young girls. If she was born in 1650, she would be fifteen, but if she was born in 1642 that would make her over twenty-one, an age when 'Mrs' was the more usual term for a woman (you needn't be married to be termed as such).

Nell had to learn her parts by rote as she couldn't read so her memory must have been astounding. Not only because she had to remember the lines for her current play but for the theatre's entire repertoire. They could be called on at any time to act in a different play. It has been suggested that she might have had her first role in Lacy's *The Old Trooper*, a send-up of Ogilby's *The Description of a Trouper*. Lacy encouraged her use of wit and helped her to memorise her parts. He also inspired her to introduce new lines into her comedic parts, though her first recorded main role was far more serious.

Nell played Cydaria, the Emperor Montezuma's daughter in Dryden's rhymed heroic drama *The Indian Emperor* performed in 1665, a sequel to *The Indian Queen*, which strived to show the conflict between love and honour. The play centred on the Spanish conquest of the Aztec Empire under Hernán Cortez. Michael Mohun, Anne Marshall and Charles Hart took the lead roles. Set twenty years after Montezuma is crowned, the emperor is pitted against Spanish invaders. Cydaria is in love with Cortez and tries to stop the bloodshed but he has to obey the orders of his king. She finally wins him over but it is too late. His general Pizarro has already ordered the attack.

The play was a success and Dryden would become a lifelong friend of Nell's, writing parts especially for her to showcase her talent. He would be contracted from 1668 to write three plays a year for the King's Company, the same year he became the first Poet Laureate, and he would always keep Nell in mind for his lead roles.

She was growing up and people were taking notice of her. She wore her reddish-brown hair in curls around her heart-shaped face with its rosy, dimpled cheeks. Dark eyelashes framed her hazel eyes. Her lips were full and would later be described as sensual. She was small and slender with the daintiest feet – a feature that would entice the King.

Nell was set to take the stage and become one of the finest actresses of her times, but her aspirations for the time being were cut short. Something devastating had made its way to England's shores: 1665 was the year of the bubonic plague. Although people were not then aware of where it came from, believing it was due to bad air or 'miasma', we now know the disease was spread by the fleas carried on black rats that had arrived in the London docklands on cargo ships from Amsterdam. In 1664, 24,000 people died of the plague in the Dutch capital alone. Dr Nathaniel Hodges believed it 'was imported to us from Holland, in packs of merchandize, and if anyone pleases to trace it further ... it came thither from Turkey in Bails of Cotton, which is a strange Preserver of the Pestilential Steams.'[33]

The disease began to show itself in London when a woman died of strange symptoms in St Giles in the Fields. It caused weakness, headaches, fever, vomiting and diarrhoea as well as extreme pain and the swelling of the lymphatic glands creating 'buboes'. Plague had often come to England over the centuries but it had been nearly thirty years since the last outbreak. In 1665 the survival rate was as low as twenty or thirty per cent. By April there were two more deaths in a poverty-stricken area not far from the King's Playhouse.

Pepys saw Nell a couple of weeks later at the rival theatre, the Duke's Playhouse, noting, 'All the pleasure of the play was, the King and my Lady Castlemayne were there; and pretty witty Nell, at the King's house, and the younger Marshall sat next us; which pleased me mightily.'[34] When the first case appeared within the city's walls, the Lord Mayor of London ordered herb-fuelled bonfires to be lit and the streets to be cleaned. No one was as yet too bothered about the disease but it was taking hold.

In May the King's Playhouse put on a production of *Love's Mistress, or the Queen's Mask* by Thomas Heywood. Nell does not seem to have been given a role this time and subsequent events would put a halt to her career for the time being. It was a worrying time as she said goodbye to some of her fellow actors who enlisted with the navy. In June the Battle of Lowestoft was fought and won off the coast of Suffolk. The Duke of York, Lord High Admiral, commanded the English fleet to its victory with resounding gunfire that could be heard in London. 'All this day by all people upon the River, and almost everywhere else hereabout were heard the guns, our two fleets for certain being engaged.'[35] Nell must have startled at such a noise, fearing for her friends and for what may come.

The long, hot summer that followed fuelled the spread of the plague. Soon houses were shut up and marked with a red cross. A note would be fixed to the door reading 'Lord have mercy on our souls'. Streets that were once clean were now mired in excrement and dirt, becoming an ideal breeding ground for the black rats that spread across the city through alleyways and buildings taking the plague with them. Poor families packed tightly in squalid living conditions in slum areas like Southwark, Finsbury and Whitechapel were the most at risk, but no one was spared the coming onslaught.

In a bid to stop the plague spreading, the theatres closed in June and gatherings of people were banned. It was ordered that dogs and cats be killed to stop the spread (although they weren't to blame): some 40,000 dogs and 200,000 cats were culled during that summer. More affected houses were daubed with the ominous red crosses and only 'nurses' were allowed in and out of the houses for a forty-day period for those who could afford them. The inhabitants were left to either recover or die.

Hart had promised Nell she would have her own dressing room but instead she was making plans to leave the city. In mid-June Nell and her mother left London, probably heading for Oxford, as other actors did. Hart joined them and must have paid for lodgings. Money was tight and it seems that payments to the King's Company were not forthcoming as later in the year they were petitioning for arrears owing.

By 20 June 168 plague deaths were recorded in one week. Around 30,000 people, including physicians, escaped the city and its sickness that summer. Those who couldn't leave and were left with no medicine and limited food supplies tried to protect themselves by camping out in green spaces or moving outside of the city to places such as Hampstead Heath. By August London had turned into a ghost town with 7,000 deaths a week. Gone was the hustle and bustle of everyday life. Few people walked the streets, and when they did they kept their distance from one another. Weeds grew in the roads and ran rampant, reclaiming gardens. The deceased were collected at night, and also by day at the height of the pestilence, in carts piled high, to be buried in mass burial pits.

At the end of June the bill of mortality – a weekly record – reported an increase in plague deaths in the city. Pepys wrote, 'The towne grows very sickly, and people to be afeard of it; there dying this last week of the plague 112, from 43 the week before.'[36] But by September he was more concerned, 'Up by 5 of the clock, mighty full of fear of an ague, but was obliged to go, and so by water, wrapping myself up warm, to the Tower, and there sent for the Weekely Bill, and find 8,252 dead in all, and of them 6,878 of the plague; which is a most dreadfull number, and shows reason to fear that the plague hath got that hold that it will yet continue among us.'[37] Evelyn as well spoke of the horrors: 'The contagion still increasing and growing now all about us ... Came home, there perishing now neere ten-thousand poore creatures weekely. However I went all along the Citty to St. James's, a dismal passage & dangerous, to see so many coffins exposed in the streetes & the streete thin of people, the shops shut up, & all in mournefull silence, as not knowing whose turn might be next.'[38] The city they left behind would see one in five Londoners die.

The King and court had also left London for Salisbury. Charles was ill for several days in September, alarming those around him, but thankfully it was not the plague. Charles told his sister, Minette, who was living in France and married to King Louis XIV's brother, Philippe I, Duke of Orléans, 'I have been troubled these few dayes past with a collique but I thank God I am now perfectly well againe ... I am goeing to make a little turne into dorset sheere for 8 or 9 days to passe away the time till I go to Oxford.'[39]

Parliament was held at Christ Church in Oxford in October and was focused on the ongoing war. The Queen was expecting their child – although unfortunately she would miscarry – and Barbara was about to give birth to a son, George, in December, whom Charles duly acknowledged. The King was anxious to return to the capital, 'where already the Plague is in effect nothing. But our women are afraide of the name of Plague, so that they must have a little time to fancy all cleere.'[40] Perhaps Nell and her mother were just as afraid. At least in December the ban was lifted on entertainments in Oxford and small-scale plays could be performed.

A severe winter saw a decline in plague victims and the death of the rats that had carried it around the city. Mortality rates decreased. The outbreak had taken its toll with around 70,000-100,000 people dying. The King made his way back to Hampton Court and then on to Whitehall at the end of January. Nell and her mother had survived and so had the King but it would be a while longer before their paths would cross, changing Nell's life forever.

Chapter Three

The Great Fire 1666-1669

Nell must have returned to city in the early months of 1666 when it was safe to do so, but the theatres would not yet be allowed to reopen. It meant nearly eighteen months of unemployment and Nell was itching to get back on the stage, going over her roles and practising her lines at home.

In March Pepys went to have a look at the playhouse:

> After dinner we walked to the King's play-house, all in dirt, they being altering of the stage to make it wider. But God knows when they will begin to act again; but my business here was to see the inside of the stage and all the tiring-rooms and machines; and, indeed, it was a sight worthy seeing. But to see their clothes, and the various sorts, and what a mixture of things there was; here a wooden-leg, there a ruff, here a hobbyhorse, there a crown, would make a man split himself to see with laughing; and particularly Lacy's wardrobe, and Shotrell's. But then again, to think how fine they show on the stage by candle-light, and how poor things they are to look now too near hand, is not pleasant at all. The machines are fine, and the paintings very pretty.[1]

While the city tried to get back to normal, the Anglo-Dutch War was continuing. At the beginning of June a ferocious and devastating four-day naval battle took place. The English fleet of fifty-six ships under the command of General Monck was outnumbered by an eighty-four strong Dutch fleet with superior guns. Thousands of Englishmen lost their lives. Eight ships were sunk with nine more captured. It was a humiliating defeat with many losses of men and young boys. Some died in battle and many more returned wounded or were taken prisoner.

War was an expensive business and one that the Crown could not sustain. Ships were destroyed, others needed repair and the sailors wanted their wages, but the King was low on funds. England could not afford to lose more men's lives, but at another skirmish on St James Day 300 Englishmen died. The Dutch, however, lost in the region of 5,000 men and for now it put an end to more hostilities. The wounded and broken returned home and walked the streets of London. Nell's heart went out to them and the plight of the soldiers would forever stay in her mind.

One of the most devastating events to affect London was yet to occur. In the early hours of 2 September, as people lay sleeping, cries of 'Fire! Fire!' rang out. In a city of wooden houses, it wasn't unusual for the peace to be broken by such a call of alarm and many rolled over in their beds and pulled the blankets tighter. This fire, however, would be the greatest conflagration to sweep across the city. Initially it started at a bake house close to Pudding Lane, near London Bridge, but it wasn't thought to be especially high risk. The Lord Mayor, Sir Thomas Bludworth, declared that 'a woman might piss it out'[2] but he was so terribly wrong.

Fanned by an easterly wind, the fire spread to adjoining houses. As people finally realised the risk and hurried from their beds, it grew out of control, fed by the tar and pitch that was stored in riverside warehouses. As the sun rose, people could see London Bridge was aflame. A gap between the buildings stopped it from spreading south and instead it spread eastwards, marching through the city and destroying all in its wake. People fled for their lives as the flames grew higher. Gathering up their children and their belongings and carrying what they could, they ran. Some tried to hastily bury their valued possessions or hide them but the flames moved too quickly, urging them on.

> All the sky was of a fiery aspect, like the top of a burning oven, and the light seen for above forty miles round for many nights. God grant that mine eyes may never behold the like, who now saw above 10,000 houses all in one flame. The noise, and cracking, and thunder, of the impetuous flames, the shrieking of the women and children, the hurry of the people, the fall of towers, houses, and churches, was like a hideous storm, and the air all about so hot and inflamed, that, at the last, one was not able to approach it.[3]

For three days London burned. Over 10,000 houses, eighty-seven parish churches and major buildings like the Royal Exchange and the Custom House went up in flames. The lead roof of Old St Pauls Cathedral melted and dropped inside the building, destroying the goods that shopkeepers had stored there for safekeeping. The chains that closed off city streets melted. Window glass, hinges, bars and church bells turned into molten metal and ran through the streets. What wasn't destroyed was irreparably damaged.

Once Charles and his brother, James, the Duke of York, heard the city was aflame, they rushed to help. Lord Chancellor Clarendon wrote that the royal brothers 'put themselves in great dangers among the burning and falling houses, to give advice and direction what was to be done, underwent as much fatigue as the meanest, and had as little sleep or rest.'[4] Covered in soot and dirt, they helped fight the fires by dowsing the flames with water from leather buckets.

The people feared that the fire was the work of a foreign enemy – the Dutch or perhaps the French – and that they would soon be invaded. Scared beyond reason, the King was forced to address what was turning into a dangerous situation for anyone suspected of being a stranger. Many wandered the streets, now homeless. Makeshift camps were set up with tents and ramshackle huts as shelter to cope with over 65,000 people. Charles rode to one of the homeless camps at Moorfields to assure the citizens of London that there was no plot. He promised that the fire was an act of God and no one was responsible. He also promised his people that they would be looked after and he made sure that rations were sent to the camps.

The official death toll came to six: an incredibly low number and one that has been questioned. It is quite possible that the figure was much higher and the deaths of the already homeless, destitute and poor were not recorded. Reports in France said, 'The letters from London speak of the terrible sights of persons burned to death and calcined limbs, making it easy to believe the terror though it cannot be exactly described. The old, tender children and many sick and helpless persons were all burned in their beds and served as fuel for the flames.'[5] So many must have perished in the flames, unnoticed and unrecorded.

It took the city some time to recover but it gradually began to return to normal. People set to work rebuilding their homes while many still lived in temporary accommodation, some moved in with relatives and others left the city. Charles embarked on restoring his capital and plans were submitted by Christopher Wren, John Evelyn, Robert Hooke, Valentine Knight and Richard Newcourt. The King wanted his city to be rebuilt with bricks and stone and appointed six commissioners including Wren to oversee the city's transformation. Although Wren would be responsible for building the new St Paul's Cathedral, none of the new plans were adhered to as property owners took matters into their own hands.

The fire had stopped before it reached Whitehall Palace and Nell's lodgings and the playhouses went unscathed, but they had been closed for months and many actors were feeling the pinch. Davenant and the Duke's Company were allowed to reopen in October with Etherege's play *Love in a Tub*. Killigrew asked the King to allow them to open their playhouse but it was opposed by the Archbishop of Canterbury until they promised they would donate one day's takings to the poor and victims of the recent tragedy. Pepys was chatting to Orange Moll when she told him that they had performed a play on 18 August. Perhaps she was mistaken or had there been a private performance and Killigrew was being penalised for it? Anyway, they were set to reopen and the female cast had been issued with new livery as the King's servants. Nell and her fellow actresses were given four yards of scarlet cloth and a quarter of a yard of velvet.

The King's Company eventually reopened with *The Maid's Tragedy* and followed it the next day with *The English Monsieur*, written by James Howard, Dryden's brother-in-law. Pepys was impressed with 'a mighty pretty play, very witty and pleasant. And the women do very well, but above all, little Nelly, that I am mightily pleased with the play, and much with the House, more than I ever expected, and very fine women.'[6] The plays may have been good but Killigrew lamented that 'the audience at his house was not above half so much as it used to be before the late fire.'[7]

Nell played Lady Wealthy, a rich widow, in *The English Monsieur,* Lacy was Mr Frenchlove and Charles Hart was her Mr Wellbred. The comedy played on their relationship but on stage these two reigned supreme as the merry couple. Everybody knew they were an item and James Howard, who knew Nell well, wrote lines such as: 'This life of mine can last no longer than my beauty; and though 'tis pleasant now – I want nothing whilst I am Mr Wellbred's mistress – yet, if his mind should change, I might e'en sell oranges for my living; and he not buy one off me to relieve me.'[8]

In four months Nell played at least seven roles. If the theatre was not packed with an eager audience, actresses had to learn new roles and practise their dancing. Nell would become famous for her comical jigs, which, Buckingham would later write, was the cause of loud applause rather than a playwright's writing.

> Besides, the author dreads the strut and mien
> Of new praised poets, having often seen
> Some of his fellows, who have write before
> When Nell danced her jig, steal to that door,
> Hear the pit clap, and with conceit of that,
> Swell, and believe themselves the Lord knows what.[9]

After such tumultuous times, the Queen's birthday celebrations at court gave some sparkle to the end of the year. Pepys had managed to get himself up into a loft space to watch the evening unfold below him.

> Anon, the house grew full, and the candles light, and the King and Queene and all the ladies sat; and it was, indeed, a glorious sight to see Mrs. Stewart in black and white lace, and her head and shoulders dressed with diamonds (only the Queen none) and the king in his rich vest of some rich silk, and silver trimming ... Presently, after the king was come in, he took the queen, and about fourteen more couple there were, and began the Bransles...After the Bransles, then to a Corant, and now and then a French dance; but that so rare that the Corants grew tiresome, that I wished it done. Only Mrs. Stewart danced mighty finely, and many French dances, specially one the King called the New Dance, which was very pretty; but upon the whole matter, the business of the dancing of itself was not extraordinary pleasing. But the clothes and sight of the persons was indeed very pleasing, and worth my coming, being never likely to see more gallantry while I live, if I should come twenty times.15 There was all the hope that the next year would be a far better one.[10]

Unfortunately, Nell would not be asked to attend – the court was no place for an orange girl turned actress – yet. She was back on stage in January 1667 for a rerun of *The Humorous Lieutenant*. Pepys lamented he had to wait for a box seat as it was so popular, though he thought it a silly play, but more delights were to come: 'Here in a box above we spied Mrs Pierce; and going out, they called us all in and brought us to Nelly, a most pretty woman, who acted the great part of Ceolia today very fine, and it did pretty well: I kissed her and so did my wife; a might pretty soul she is … Knipp made us stay in a box and see the dancing preparatory for tomorrow for "The Goblins", a play of Suckling's not acted these twenty-five years; and so away thence, pleased with this sight also, and specially of kissing of Nell.'[11]

Nell now had friends in high places and was invited to the Earl of Rochester's wedding on 29 January 1667. Rochester was a playwright, poet and all-round rake. Burnet described him as 'a lawless and wretched mountebank; his delight was to haunt the stews, to debauch women, to write filthy songs and lewd pamphlets; he spent his time in gossiping with the maids of honour, broils with men of letters, the receiving of insults, the giving of blows.'[12] His marriage to Elizabeth Malet, an heiress, came years after he first abducted her, and he spent time in the Tower for this affront. But Elizabeth had stayed true to her erstwhile kidnapper and refused to marry anyone her family chose until they finally gave in and consented to her marriage to the earl.

It was at Rochester's wedding that George Villiers, 2nd Duke of Buckingham, approached Nell about taking a role in his adaptation of Fletcher's play, *The Chances*. Buckingham was a prominent member of Charles' Merry Gang. Another notorious rake and womaniser, he had been raised with the King since his father's assassination. The first duke had been one of James I's favourites and Lord Admiral under Charles I until his death in 1628. Never popular, a disgruntled army officer, John Felton, stabbed him at the Greyhound Pub in Portsmouth. He cried out 'Villian!' before he collapsed. Such was the public's dislike of the duke, that Felton was lauded as a hero.

The first duke's children, a daughter, Mary, and his two sons, George and Francis, came under the care of Charles I. Mary was sent to live with the Earl of Pembroke whilst George and Francis were brought up at court. It was later said that it was hard for Buckingham to remember he wasn't a prince. Always by Charles' side in exile, he returned to England to marry

Mary Fairfax, the daughter of Thomas Fairfax, 3rd Lord Fairfax of Cameron, a Parliamentarian commander, much to Charles' disgust. But he was soon in trouble for his suspected plotting and spent some time in the Tower.

With Charles' restoration, Buckingham returned to favour, although the King did not initially welcome him with open arms. He was never quite sure whether to trust him or not and it made their relationship fractious. Buckingham was ever the schemer and in February 1667 he spent time in the Tower for his plotting and having cast the King's horoscope to predict his death. Charles would soon forgive him even though he would continue his intrigues. In the *Life of George Villiers*, he is described: 'For his person, he was the glory of the age and any court wherever he came. Of the most graceful and charming mien and behaviour; a strong, tall and active body, all of which gave lustre to the ornaments of his mind; of an admirable wit and excellent judgement; … he was courteous and affable to all; of a compassionate nature; ready to forgive and forget injuries … but when he was provoked by the malice of some and ingratitude of others, he might show that a good-natured man might have an ill-natured muse.'[13]

He would become a part of Nell's life, just as good at mimicry and clowning around as she was. Pepys thought Nell and Buckingham might have been lovers but it was just gossip. Rochester was also rumoured to be one of Nell's lovers and Etherege's scurrilous poem *The Lady of Pleasure* considered that Buckhurst had allowed her to serve other men.

> To Buckhurst thus resigned in friendly wise,
> He takes her swinge and sometimes lends her thighs
> To bestial Buckingham's transcendent prick
> And sometimes witty Wilmot had a lick.[14]

In the Victoria and Albert museum is a pamphlet entitled *A Genuine letter from the Earl of Rochester to Nell Gwyn, Copied from an original manuscript in the French King's library*. Although it has been debated as to whether Rochester wrote it or part of it, it includes a poem to Nell at the age of fifteen and in which the author tells of their love affair.

> Nine times one night I plumb'd the dark abyss,
> And, like Leander, cross'd new seas of bliss.
> So close thou clung'st, so eager in the joy,
> Rapture fresh rapture met, nor knew no cloy.[15]

The historian Burnet, never a fan of Nell, said that Charles 'never treated her with the decencies of a mistress, but rather with the lewdness of a prostitute; as she had been indeed to a great many,' but this was blatantly untrue. If Nell had had many lovers, there would be more stories, more evidence, and there isn't. Especially once she was with the King, no other man would do.

Nell's next comic role would commence on 2 March 1667. Dryden had written *Secret Love or the Maiden Queen*, with Nell in mind for the lead role of Florimel, a breeches wearing wit, 'the most comicall that ever was made for woman'.[16] Her description in the play is that of Nell to a tee: 'an Oval Face, clear Skin, hazel Eyes, thick brown Eye-brows and Hair … a turn'd up Nose … a full neather Lip, an out-mouth … the bottom of your cheeks a little blub, and two dimples when you smile; for your stature 'tis well (enough), and for your wit twas given you by one that knew it had been thrown away upon an ill face.'[17]

Pepys was over the moon about the performance and wrote:

> After dinner with my wife, to the King's House to see The Maiden Queen, a new play of Dryden's, mightily commended for the regularity of it, and the starin and wit; and, the truth is, there is a comical part done by Nell, which is Florimel, that I can never hope to see the like done again, by man or woman. The King and the Duke of York were at the play. But so great performance of a comical part was never, I believe, in the world before as Nell do this, both as a mad girl, then most and best of all when she comes in like a young gallant; and hath the motions and carriage of a spark the most that I ever saw any man have. It makes me, I confess, admire her.[18]

High praise indeed from Pepys who would later not be quite so enthusiastic, but he loved the performance so much he saw it several times and even bought a copy of the play when it was printed.

At the same time, Moll Davis, an actress from the Duke's Company, was in *The English Princess*. Both Moll and Nell had come from humble backgrounds, and both sought to become the country's finest actresses, so it was inevitable there would be some rivalry between them. Pepys suggested Moll was the illegitimate daughter of Thomas Howard, the 3rd Earl of Berkshire, but others thought she was just the offspring of a common blacksmith and was only giving herself airs.

Moll had been acting since she was a child and now boarded with Sir William Davenant, owner of the Duke's Playhouse. The gossiping diarist Pepys thought she was a better dancer than Nell after seeing her in the play, and felt 'there is no comparison between Nell's dancing the other day at the King's house in boy's clothes and this, this being infinitely beyond the other.'[19]

As many an actress before and after her, Moll soon came to the King's attention. Her rendition of 'My Lodging it is on the Cold Ground' in the play *The Rivals* tugged on the sovereign's heartstrings. Mournfully she sang:

> My lodging it is on the cold ground,
> And oh! very hard is my fare,
> But that which troubles me most is
> The unkindness of my dear.
> Yet still I cry, 'Oh turn, love,'
> And Prithee, love turn to me,
> For thou art the man that I long for,
> And alack! what remedy?[20]

Then she curled up and fell asleep. It was said she sang quite 'so touchingly that the song raised her from the cold ground to the royal couch.'[21] Her performance saw her escorted up the back stairs to the King's closet, but not everyone was so impressed with Moll. People felt that she flaunted her new-found popularity and was vulgar and greedy, even upsetting the Queen with her provocative dancing during a court performance.

Nell's and Moll's supporters often took sides and Nell was often taunted and abused by Moll's followers for taking off her rival in *The Mad Couple,* another play where she and Charles Hart took the main roles of Mirida and Philidor. Pepys thought *The Mad Couple* was quite ordinary but that Nell's and Hart's 'mad parts are excellently done, but especially hers.'[22]

She mimicked Moll's plaintive song while being chased around the stage by a chubby Pinguister played by John Lacy.

> My lodging is on the cold boards,
> And wonderful hard is my fare,
> But that which troubles me most is
> The fatness of my dear.
> Yet still I cry, Oh melt, love,
> And I pr'ythee now melt apace,
> For thou art the man I should long for
> If 'twere not for thy grease.[23]

First round to Nelly, who then had the crowd roaring with laughter as Pinguister rolled around the stage after her as she rolled away even faster, flashing her ample petticoats.

The Mad Couple was the play that attracted Lord Buckhurst, her next beau. He was one of Charles' 'Merry Gang', that group of notorious rakes hell-bent on entertaining themselves while also being patrons of the arts. Heavy drinking parties, debauched sex and the creation of witty poetry was all in an evening's entertainment. Whilst the king did not join in on their wildest evenings, he was certainly involved with the group, and its members were some of his closest friends. Something they all had in common was their taking of mistresses, but the king drew the line at their more outrageous behaviour and had at times to reprimand them, fine them or, for the worst offences, have them taken to the Tower to cool their heels.

Lady Dorothy Howard, one of the Duchess of York's maids-in-waiting, had the measure of one of the most notorious of the gang, John Wilmot, Earl of Rochester, and when his attention turned to Anne Temple, she wrote, warning her: 'Lord Rochester is undoubtedly the most witty man in England; but he is also the most unprincipled. He is nothing but a danger to our sex; and that to such a degree that no woman listens to him three times without irretrievably losing her reputation … In the meantime nothing is more dangerous than the creepy way he lays hold of your mind. He applauds your taste, submits to your feelings, and even though he himself does not believe a single word of what he is saying, he makes you believe it all.'[24]

All of these men enjoyed the theatre and the pleasures of its actresses. Some would say they were harmless if not unruly, but some of the girls' patrons were not so pleasant. Being an actress came with the risk of dealing with men who thought the girls nothing more than whores. Rebecca (Beck) Marshall, another actress with the King's Playhouse, had been attacked by one Mark Trevor who 'assaulted her violently in a coach and after many horrid oaths and threats that he would be revenged of her for complaining to my Lord Chamberlain formerly of him, pursu'd her with his sword in his hand.'[25] She had to flee into a house for safety while he continued to swear at her and break windows. Then in 1667, Sir Hugh Middleton had made some suggestive remarks about the women in the company and when he appeared backstage Rebecca berated him for his ill language. He told her she was lying and if she continued he would kick her and get his footman to kick her too. Rebecca was frightened and asked the King for his protection but nothing could stop her being waylaid and attacked by a man Middleton hired to smear excrement in her face and hair.

There was little Charles could do to prevent this sort of behaviour, but, as the King's servants, the actresses should have been safeguarded. Proclamations were made to try to stop members of the audience going backstage. One in 1664 read 'no person of what quality soever do presume to enter at the door of the attiring house, but such as do belong to the company and are employed by them,'[26] but it would not stop the clamour of people who were desperate to see the actresses and vie for their attention.

For now, though, the King had his mind on other women. He was devastated when his favourite diversion in the form of Frances Stuart eloped with her beau, the Duke of Richmond. She had tired of the King's attention and wanted to marry but no permission had been forthcoming. She begged the Queen to forgive her for flirting so shamelessly with the King and asked for her help to escape from court. At the end of March she wrapped herself warmly against the stormy night and left Whitehall. She made her way across London Bridge to The Bear at the Bridge Foot tavern on the southern side of the river, where the duke was waiting with a carriage to take her to his ancestral home of Cobham Hall. There they were married, at the beginning of April. Charles vowed he would never allow her or her husband into his presence ever again. He was heartbroken and wretched, taking it out on everyone around him, especially the Queen, who had supported Frances' flight.

On 18 April 1667 the King, in an effort to cheer himself up, requested a performance of *Secret Love or the Maiden Queen* at court. He paid £10 7s for Nell's costume and 'rhinegraves' – breeches that were split to show off a tantalising glimpse of the thigh. Theatrical fashion was nothing if not daring, revealing glimpses of a woman's body that were not usually seen. The prologue to Thyestes mentions:

> She that Dances jilts the very eyes,
> Allowing only these Discoveries,
> A neat silk Leg, and pair of Holland Thighs.[27]

The King wasn't the only one admiring Nell's body. Mayday was a day of celebration and Pepys was delighted when on his walk to Westminster he spied 'many milkmaids, with their garlands on their pails, dancing with a fiddler before them; and saw pretty Nell standing at her lodgings' door in Drury Lane in her smock sleeves and bodice, looking upon one; she seemed a mighty pretty creature.'[28] And he was not the only one who had become enamoured of her.

That summer, after she appeared in Sir Robert Howard's comedy, *The Surprisal*, Nell gave in to Charles Sackville, Lord Buckhurst, who took her to off to Epsom to consummate their affair. Her liaison with Charles Hart was over.

> Yet Hart more manners had, than not to tender,
> When noble Buckhurst begged him to surrender.
> Her saw her roll the stage from side to side
> And, through her drawers the powerful charm descried.
> "Take her my lord," quoth Hart, "since you're so mean
> To take a player's leavings for your queen."[29]

Nell's brother-in-law, Cassells, had been arrested and her mother was found drunk in Drury Lane – definitely not for the first time, but it was embarrassing for Nell as she was trying to rise in the world. Buckhurst was a way for her to rise, to be cared for and be looked after, but he was no saint either. He was another one of Charles' friends who had literally got away with murder. In 1662 Sackville and his brother, Edward, robbed and murdered a tanner named Hoppy. In their defence, they said that they had thought Hoppy was a highwayman. They were convicted of manslaughter, but typically of the King, they were pardoned a week later.

Nell and Buckhurst shared their house with Charles Sedley and it was rumoured he also shared their bed. Sedley was no shrinking violet. In a well quoted incident of the time, Buckhurst, Sir Thomas Ogle and Sedley spent a day drinking at the Cock Inn and took their antics out on to the balcony where Sedley 'showed his nakedness – and abusing of scripture and as it were from thence preaching a mountebank sermon from the pulpit, saying that there he had to sell such a pouder as should make all the cunts in town run after him, 1000 people standing underneath to see and hear him, and that being done he took a glass of wine and washed his prick in it and then drank it off, and then took another and drank the King's health.'[30] He was fined 2000 marks. It was one of those stories that grew with the retelling. One version had them dining on six dishes of meat served by six naked women. Another that the mob, so scandalised and disgusted, rushed the doors of the tavern and it was only after 'a long and desperate fight' that Sedley, Buckhurst and Ogle 'were rescued from its clutches; indeed all three nearly lost their lives as they had successfully lost their characters.'[31]

Nell was enjoying a madcap summer with some of the most notorious rakes of the time. They were sometimes joined by Sedley's daughter, the nine-year-old Catherine, who would grow up to become the Duke of York's mistress but for now may have put a rein on their excesses and provided some semblance of normality in an otherwise chaotic few weeks.

While they were in Epsom they heard that the English fleet had been attacked at Chatham. The Dutch arrived off the coast of Kent in June. They took the fort at Sheerness and sailed on up the Medway to burst through the chain protecting the entrance to the royal boatyard. Charles' flagship, the *Royal Charles*, was captured as well as the *Unity* and the *Royal Oak*, *Royal James* and *Loyal London* plus ten smaller ships were burnt in the water. People feared a Dutch invasion but the fleet withdrew after the damage was done, taking with it the *Royal Charles* in a final humiliating act. People lambasted the King for being slow to rally England's defences, and also because it was rumoured he had sat out the whole ordeal at Barbara's house with others who were 'all mad in hunting of a poor moth.'[32] On 21 July the Treaty of Breda was signed, signalling the end of the second Anglo-Dutch War and for a time there would be peace in England.

Pepys may have been a bit late with the gossip in July but he was troubled by finding out 'my Lord Buckhurst hath got Nell away from the King's house, lies with her, and gives her £100 a year, so she hath sent her parts to the house and will act no more.'[33] Buckhurst must certainly have had a hold on Nell to convince her to leave the theatre. Perhaps she thought he would set her up for life. Pepys took a trip to Epsom – probably just to see for himself – where he heard 'that my Lord Buckhurst and Nelly are lodged at the next house, and Sir Charles Sidly with them: and keep a merry house. Poor girl! I pity her; but more the loss of her at the King's house.'[34]

When the theatres reopened in August there was no sign of Nell. Pepys was not happy with the play *The Customs of the Country* that was showing but was filled in on the gossip by Mary Knepp – once Pepys's lover – who told him that Nell was still kept by Lord Buckhurst.

However, something happened between the couple in August that resulted in Nell returning to London. Whatever the quarrel was over, Nell was done with her lord although they would remain friends. Pepys noted that there was some ill-feeling towards the young actress who, on her return to the King's Playhouse, was being spurned by her fellow actors. He wrote in his diary: 'I had a great deal of discourse with Moll; who tells us that Nell is already left by my Lord Buckhurst, and that he makes sport of her, and swears she hath had all she could get of him; and Hart, her great admirer, now hates her; and that she is very poor, and hath lost Lady Castlemaine, who was her great friend also; but she is come to the House, but is neglected by them all.'[35] But this was just gossip. Buckhurst would be close to Nell throughout her life, even though the king would later take no chances of them rekindling their relationship and send him off on random diplomatic missions.

Hart may have missed her privately but he needed her professionally. They were the archetypal mad couple and they worked well together. He had put a lot into her training and it must have smarted that she would give it all up so easily. Regardless of his personal feelings, he had to acknowledge her return, as did her fellow actors who soon rallied round her. It was not long before she was acting as Cydaria in *The Indian Emperor*, though she fell out with actress Rebecca Marshall who called her Buckhurst's whore, to which she retorted, 'I was but one man's whore, though I was brought up in a bawdy house ... and you are a whore to three or four though a Presbyter's praying daughter.'[36]

Barbara, the most 'vicious and ravenous'[37] was now having an affair with Charles Hart. Nell's mentor and ex-lover had moved on, as had she. Rochester, who it was said frequented brothels with Barbara, wrote of her insatiable appetite:

> When she has jaded quite
> Her almost boundless appetite
> She'll still drudge on in tasteless vice
> As if she sinned for exercise.[38]

When the court left for a visit to Tunbridge Wells in Kent, Nell followed, as did her rival at the Duke's Playhouse, Moll Davis. Tunbridge Wells was known for its healing waters, which, it was claimed, could aid fertility as well as many other ailments. In 1606 Lord North had discovered a chalybeate spring there. It became a popular spa retreat loved by Charles' mother and Queen Catherine, but it was also called '*les eaux de scandale*' by the French ambassador. It was a place of clandestine liaison, and the resulting pregnancies were not just due to the reddish water's healing properties.

Both girls were looking for a rich patron and they were egged on by high profile courtiers like Rochester and Buckingham. Buckingham especially believed the King should divorce his barren Queen and he was concerned that Barbara, who was his cousin, had way too much clout and should be replaced. She did him no favours and he thought her influence might be negated by interesting the King in more pliable women, in his mind anyway –namely actresses.

Buckingham also sought to bring down the Lord Chancellor. Clarendon had been blamed for many things over the years; the Duke of York's marriage to his daughter, the selling of Dunkirk to France, arranging for Charles to marry a barren Queen and allowing them to have a Catholic ceremony. The duke and his friend the Earl of Bristol had spent many years looking for a way to bring him down and were instrumental in previously having Clarendon impeached. He was charged with causing the union of the royal couple 'without any settled Agreement in what manner the Rights of Marriage should be performed,' and of subjecting the King to the 'suspicion of having been married in his own Dominions by a Romish Priest.'[39] But Clarendon had been the King's faithful servant for many years and Charles was furious at

Buckingham's meddling. He protected his Lord Chancellor and banned the duke from court for a time.

Now after the debacle at Chatham and the loss of the King's flagship to the Dutch, Buckingham saw a way to finally get rid of the Lord Chancellor. He amassed such support that the King was convinced in October to impeach Clarendon on seventeen charges. Not everyone supported the Lord Chancellor's fall from grace and the House of Lords refused to accept the charges against him, but Buckingham was still pushing for a trial – which could end in Clarendon's execution – and not to give him any further chances. The Lord Chancellor fled to France where he would remain in exile for the rest of his life.

With Clarendon gone, Buckingham became the King's chief adviser and he had Nell in his sights for the King's new mistress. Nell may have got close to the King at Tunbridge Wells, but on her return to London she had rehearsals and new plays to learn. In October she played Flora in Richard Rhodes' *Flora's Vagaries* with Mrs Knepp as Otrante, Mohun as Alberto and Burt as Francisco.

Pepys saw her there, though he had been to Davenant's playhouse first because they were showing a new play, *The Coffee-house*. But he could not get in and so instead went to the King's Playhouse:

> and there, going in, met with Knepp, and she took us up into the tireing-rooms: and to the women's shift, where Nell was dressing herself, and was all unready, and is very pretty, prettier than I thought. And so walked all up and down the house above, and then below into the scene-room, and there sat down, and she gave us fruit and here I read the questions to Knepp, while she answered me, through all her part of "Flora's Figary's," which was acted to-day. But, Lord! to see how they were both painted would make a man mad, and did make me loath them; and what base company of men comes among them, and how lewdly they talk! and how poor the men are in clothes, and yet what a shew they make on the stage by candle-light, is very observable. But to see how Nell cursed, for having so few people in the pit, was pretty; the other house carrying away all the people at the new play, and is said, now-a-days, to have generally most company, as being better players. By and by into the pit, and there saw the play, which is pretty good.'[40]

Nell had cursed for the lack of an audience. If the play wasn't popular it would mean a new play would be performed the next day with immediate rehearsals and the learning of new lines.

The King was quite taken with his little actresses and Thomas Chiffinch, his procurer, had taken both Nell and Moll up the back stairs for private liaisons with Charles. Nell was friends with Thomas' brother, William, who took over the role, and his wife, but the story goes that Nell asked the King for £500 a year which was declined and instead Charles took Moll as his regular mistress.

On a visit to the theatre in January 1668 Mrs Knepp sat next to Pepys and his wife. She was not impressed with Moll. He noted after talking to her:

> That she did sit near the players of the Duke's house; among the rest, Miss Davis, who is the most impertinent slut, she says, in the world; and the more, now the King do show her countenance; and is reckoned his mistress, even to the scorne of the whole world; the King gazing on her, and my Lady Castlemayne being melancholy and out of humour, all the play, not smiling once. The King, it seems, hath given her a ring of L700, which she shews to everybody, and owns that the King did give it her; and he hath furnished a house for her in Suffolke Street most richly, which is a most infinite shame. It seems she is a bastard of Colonell Howard, my Lord Berkshire, and that he do pimp to her for the King, and hath got her for him; but Pierce says that she is a most homely jade as ever she saw, though she dances beyond anything in the world. She tells me that the Duchesse of Richmond do not yet come to the Court, nor hath seen the King, nor will not, nor do he own his desire of seeing her; but hath used means to get her to Court, but they do not take.[41]

So Charles gave Moll a house in Suffolk Street and an expensive ring worth far more than the £500 a year that Nell had asked for, yet Nell was not giving up without a fight. One day, on hearing that her rival was to dine privately with the King, she invited Moll to afternoon tea. Under the pretext of a cordial tête-à-tête, Nell planned to make sure she and the King had a night to remember. Aphra Behn, a playwright and former spy, lived close by in Lincoln Inn Fields and she and Nell would become firm friends. Behn gave Nell a powdered substance, some jalap weed, as a special 'treat' for her rival. Nell gleefully slipped it into some sweetmeats she offered the unsuspecting Moll. This was no extra spice but a strong laxative that would cause a rather startling reaction!

The poor girl had a very unpleasant evening with the King, to Nell's great mirth and delight. Some sources say Moll was pregnant with the King's child at the time. The one daughter we know she gave birth to was Lady Mary Tudor, who may have been this child, although her date of birth is more commonly thought to be in 1673. Perhaps this was a pregnancy that didn't go full-term. Hopefully not due to Nell's prank!

On 20 February 1668 Pepys saw her speaking the prologue and epilogue of *The Great Favourite, or the Duke of Lerma* by Sir Robert Howard, one of the company's shareholders and a man who would later be one of Nell's trustees. He was also brother to James Howard in whose play, *The English Monsieur*, Nell had acted, and another of his siblings Thomas was purported to be the father of another of the king's mistresses, Moll Davis.

The play was a controversial one and Pepys was worried how it would come across when he attended and saw the King there. He noted that it 'was designed to reproach our King with his mistresses, that I was troubled for it, and expected it should be interrupted; but it ended all well, which salved all.'[42] The epilogue again is a personal anecdote:

> I know you in your hearts
> Hate serious plays – as I hate serious parts
> To trouble us with thoughts and state designs,
> A melancholy plot tied with strong lines!
> I had not the least part today, you see:
> Troth, he has neither writ for you nor me.[43]

In April Nell was watching Etherege's *She Would If She Could*, sitting in a box with a companion, a relative of Buckingham's, next to the King. Charles and his brother, James, chatted to her during the course of the play and when they left for dinner, invited her along. They spent two hours dining, drinking and conversing, although James wasn't on best form with Nell calling him a 'dismal Jimmie'. Too soon Nell had to leave. She had an early start the next morning with rehearsals for a new play. Charles called for the bill but neither he nor James had the money to pay, leaving Nell to cough up for their evening. She couldn't resist quoting the King with his favourite expression 'Odds fish!' and went on to say, 'this is the poorest company I ever was in.'[44]

The theatre world was sent into turmoil when Sir William Davenant died in April. He passed away in London shortly after *The Man's the Master*, was first performed. The diarist John Aubrey watched as his coffin of walnut wood was carried from the playhouse to Westminster Abbey where 'his grave is in the south cross aisle and on it is written (in imitation of Ben Jonson): "O rare Sir Will. Davenant".'[45] Killigrew soon acquired the rights to the play and Nell found herself in rehearsals for the role of Lucilla, a role that Moll Davis had previously played.

London faced more turmoil at Easter 1668. Known as the Bawdy House riots, the brothels and bawdy houses of the East End were looted and destroyed by hundreds of young men unhappy with the King's recent proclamation on private worship and enforcement of the Act of Uniformity. They were fed up with the double standards at court and the debauchery and licentiousness that the Restoration had brought with it.

Prostitutes and street girls were attacked. Barbara Villiers, who some considered the greatest whore of all, was also a focus. A satirical pamphlet, *The Poor Whores Petition*, addressed her as 'the most splendid, illustrious, serene, and eminent lady of pleasure,' and called on her to help out her fellow 'sisters'. Another pamphlet written in response, *The Gracious Answer*, added further insult to injury. There were calls for Charles to give up his mistress, who was draining the treasury dry, but he would not be forced to relinquish her, even though by now their relationship was waning. He made a point of giving her Berkshire House but their time was nearly done. The King had tired of her ranting and raging and her insatiable appetite. Nell was in the ascendant and made Barbara know it by making everyone laugh at her imitations of her.

Another woman the King adored was back at court but she was no rival to Nell. Frances, now the Duchess of Richmond, had returned to visit the Queen who had suffered another miscarriage. Frances lodged at Somerset House with her husband but soon caught smallpox, marring her pretty face and deterring the King's visits. Still he was known to slip out of Whitehall late at night to see the woman he once loved to distraction.

It was a busy year for Nell at the theatre and she did not have time to worry about who the King was sleeping with. She played Samira in *The Surprisal*, Lady Wealthy in *The English Monsieur* in March and April, and Victoria in Sedley's first play *The Mulberry Garden* in May, a role that was written specifically for her. In June she played the role of Donna Jacinta in Dryden's new comedy, *An Evening's Love,* and said that an ordinary lover was only good 'to be admitted to pass my time with while a better comes; to be the lowest step in my staircase for a knight to mount upon him, and a lord upon him, and a duke upon him, till I get as high as I can climb.'[46] A prophetic nod to how high she would climb herself.

She acted in Flecknoe's *Damoiselles á la Mode* in September – a play which didn't go down too well but prompted Flecknoe to write a poem in a sort-of-apology to Nell:

> She is pretty, and she knows it;
> She is witty, and she sows it;
> And besides that she's so witty,
> And so little and so pretty,
> She has a hundred other parts
> For to take and conquer hearts.[47]

In October she took the role of Angelo, the good angel, in *The Virgin Martyr*. Pepys saw Nell backstage with Rebecca Marshall, commenting: 'Their confidence! And how many men do hover about them as soon as they come off stage, and how confident they are in their talk!'[48] Nell's friendship and rivalry with Rebecca would have its ups and downs. She would later even call in the Lord Chamberlain's men to arrest Orange Moll for abusing her colleague 'to the disturbance of his majesties actors and committing other misdemeanours.'[49]

Nell and Mary Knepp spoke the prologue of Ben Jonson's play *Cataline's Conspiracy* with Nell dressed rather fetchingly in an Amazonian habit carrying a bow and arrows with a crested helmet on top of her curly locks. She finally got her own dressing room and was given new costumes. Her rise in the theatre made her a star, one whom audiences flocked to see.

Then there was the excitement of command performances at Whitehall when the troupe would put on a play especially for the King. It was a real treat for the actors and actresses. All their needs were covered and their retiring rooms were luxurious, supplied with tables, chairs, candlesticks, chamber pots, hangings, curtains and 'one Looking glasse of twenty-seven Inches for the Woemen Comedians.'[50] They would be spoiled with the best food and drink after, on one occasion running to 'Twelve Quarts of Sack, twelve Quarts of Clarett ... Eight Gallons of Beere ... six dishes of Meate, twelves loaves of white Bread, loaves of Brown Bread.'[51] There was no expense spared when it came to the King's evening entertainment.

Nell was becoming much closer to the merry monarch and she showed it in the way she dressed. We don't know if Charles eventually gave in and allowed her the £500 a year she wanted but he certainly began to give her presents, including a silver snuffbox in the shape of a book engraved with *Ouid de arte amada* – Ovid, *The Art of Love* – and soon set her up in a house in Newman's Row, ten minutes away from the theatre.

Newman's Row was in an up and coming area for the rich close to Lincoln Inn Fields. It was known for duelling, robberies and even executions, although Nell's house was in the poorest part of the area close to a narrow street more like her childhood lodgings in Coal Yard Alley. 'Nell Gwin, beinge asked why shee removed from ye good ayre in Lincolsin fields to worse neare Whit-hall, replyed shee had but on (one) good friend in ye world & shee loved to get as neare him as she could.'[52] Nell was determined to be closer to the King and make herself available. Once she had him in her grasp, she was not letting go for anyone.

The King spent many evenings in her humble abode as their relationship blossomed. It was obvious to all that Charles was now quite taken with her, and for those who witnessed their new attraction and hated Barbara she was a breath of fresh air. Where the public detested the King's grasping mistress, 'it was with relief that the public learned that the King had taken a mistress from the people, the transcendently beautiful and good-natured Nell Gwynn, who was lustily cheered in the streets.'[53] The people loved her and showed it.

Nell played Pulcharia in *The Sisters* at the beginning of the year but took a break to see *The Island Princess*, where Pepys saw her. She would always turn to a good performance at the theatre at times to cheer herself up and she enjoyed the excitement of watching her friends and her rivals from the Duke's Company. Pepys, once enthralled by Nell, now began to talk about her with some disdain. 'We sat in the upper box and the jade Nell came and sat in the next box: a bold, merry slut, who lay laughing there upon people, and with a comrade of hers of the Duke's House, that came to see the play.'[54] It seems that her move from actress to mistress had upset him, despite the fact that he was regularly unfaithful to his wife.

Charles enjoyed time away from the city and Newmarket was one place where he and Nell could escape to. That spring they headed off to the town where Charles could be more himself. Nell shared his love of horses – more for the gambling than anything else – but was a terrible rider.

By May 1669 Nell was in rehearsals for Dryden's new play *Tyrannic Love*. She was to play Valeria, a Roman princess. For the finale she tragically stabbed herself to death and was carried off stage, but before she got to the wings she would jump up and rail at the person carrying her, shouting 'Hold! Are you mad, you damn confounded dog! I am rise to speak the epilogue!' The epilogue she spoke was personal. It started:

> I come, kind gentlemen, strange news to tell ye:
> I am the ghost of poor departed Nelly
> Sweet ladies, be not frightened, I'll be civil,
> I'm what I was, a harmless little devil.

She then refers to her dislike of serious parts:

> To tell you true, I walk because I die
> Out of my calling, in a tragedy.
> O poet, damned dull poet, who could prove
> So senseless to make Nelly die for love!

And ended with:

> As for my epitaph when I am gone,
> I'll trust no poet, but will write my own:
> "Here Nelly lies, who, though she lived a slattern,
> Yet died a princess, acting in Saint Cattern.[55]

The role 'so captivated the King, who was present the first Night of the Play, by the humourous Turns she gave it, that his Majesty, when she had done, went behind the Scenes and carried her off to an Entertainment that night.'[56] Charles would ever be impressed by a good performance and the carrying off would inevitably end in his bed.

Nell was an actress and not a lady so she never received the invitations to court as other ladies did. Nell was more likely to enter by the back stairs not the grand hall, but she did attend a banquet when Prince Cosimo of Tuscany visited. Even he was taken with the young woman who he saw 'quaff a great goblet of canary.'[57] She was fast becoming a permanent fixture in the King's life. In that summer of 1669 Charles told the Queen he had a cold and would be staying in bed. Queen Catherine thought she would check on him and visited his chambers early one morning. Seeing the King was not ailing too badly she turned to go but spotted one of Nell's little slippers peeking out from under the bed. 'I will not stay for fear the pretty fool that owns that little slipper might take cold,' she told him. She had become resigned to the King's affairs, but knew that even if she did not share his passion she did share his love.

Yet that summer was all about Charles and Nell. He was besotted with her and she with him. He might play the field but Nell was always faithful and would take no other man to her bed. And, of course, the inevitable would soon happen. By the end of the year Nell was pregnant with her first child – the son of the King.

Chapter Four

A French Rival 1670-1672

Nell was keeping her sovereign warm at night and was expecting his child. Whether she felt any sadness for the Queen who had failed to give the King an heir we will never know, but her friend Buckingham had his own plans to rid Charles of his barren wife.

In March 1670 a ground-breaking bill was introduced to Parliament that would allow Lord Roos, a Whig politician, to divorce his wife and remarry. Only the church before now could grant a divorce. If one then wanted to remarry, Parliament had to agree. There was a huge debate that Charles listened to and appeared to be considering. The Duke of Buckingham took this as a sign that the King was seriously debating divorcing the Queen. He came up with the idea of his own bill – a Royal Divorce and Remarriage Bill – but Charles would not support it.

Buckingham had also come up with the appalling idea of kidnapping Catherine and seeing her transported to an American plantation. Her desertion would give Charles grounds for divorce and she could live out her life in obscurity. Charles would not hear of it and told Buckingham, 'it would be a wicked thing to make a poor woman miserable only because she is my wife, and has no children by me, which is no fault of hers.'[1] Nell thought Buckingham was mad and told him so. She knew she would never be raised as high but by getting rid of the Queen it would pave the way for someone else, someone who might negatively influence her comfortable relationship with Charles.

On 8 May 1670 she gave birth to the King's son, Charles. Her mother and sister would have helped during her lying-in, plus a woman, not known, from the court who could confirm a royal birth. Well-wishers flocked to her house to see the new child and bring gifts for them both. Prince Cosimo, who had since become the Grand Duke of Tuscany, sent a layette and there were toys and silverware from visiting ambassadors. The King was ecstatic about this new member of his ever-growing family, and for Nell it meant her future was secure. The King would always provide for his son, no matter what happened with his mistress.

Nell had not acted for several months, and now she was enamoured of the King, her acting days were numbered. She was safe in the knowledge that the King cared for her and spent much of his time with her. She knew there were other dalliances, but she was now his main mistress, although there would be someone who would soon enter their lives and upset Nell's stability. The life of a mistress, even the King's mistress, was never going to be completely secure.

Charles had been negotiating a secret treaty with Louis XIV and to further the negotiations his baby sister, Henrietta Anne, whom he affectionately called Minette, was making the voyage from France back to England – a place she had left as a baby when she was smuggled out of England for her safety during the English Civil War. She had been home once but it had been nine years since she had stepped foot on English soil. At the end of May she arrived and was first escorted to Dover Castle by Charles, James, the Duke of Monmouth (Charles' eldest illegitimate son) and Prince Rupert of the Rhine. It was a happy occasion but one Nell could not be part of.

Minette had a controlling and mean-tempered husband, the King of France's brother, Philippe, Duke of Orleans. The flamboyant duke, who enjoyed dressing in women's clothes and taking male lovers, treated Minette with contempt. She had become close to the French king and Philippe was jealous of their intimacy, even though he was the unfaithful one. It was said that Minette and Louis were lovers and that her first child, a daughter, was the king's. The duke had grown up in the shadow of the sun king and his jealousy was a bitter and twisted thing. Louis XIV had since moved on to another mistress but Minette's husband would never trust the English king's sister and made her life a misery.

It had been difficult to get the duke to agree to allow Minette to visit her brother in England. He was unaware that it wasn't just a family visit, and, ever controlling, only allowed her to stay for three days at first. Negotiations began but then the French king granted her permission to stay for ten or twelve days more. His brother could no longer argue, and for a time Minette was free and with her family.

Charles' sister was tasked with seeing that the secret treaty between her home country and the land she had come to love was agreed.

The pact included a plan for further hostilities with the Dutch. France was to attack by land, England by sea. Charles promised to supply 6,000 troops and fifty warships. Louis would provide thirty ships, all to be under the command of the King's brother, James, the Duke of York. For the king of England's ongoing support, Louis would pay him 3,000,000 livres (around £120,000) for every year of the war. But that was not all the treaty contained. The reason for so much secrecy was that Charles agreed to convert to Catholicism and slowly return England to the old faith. Louis would pay him a lump sum of one million livres when he made the declaration – the date being 'left absolutely to his own pleasure,'[2] – and a further one million livres were to be paid three months after. Charles would receive a vast sum. That agreed, the secret treaty of Dover was signed on 1 June.

Unlike Barbara who dabbled in politics, Nell wasn't overtly political and would not have involved herself in the King's business, but her house was a meeting place – a place for discussion as well as for pleasure – and we can be sure that the King debated the merits of the treaty at her house behind closed doors with the French ambassador, Colbert de Croissy. Nell provided refreshments and saw that the men were not disturbed. Whitehall, with its maze of corridors and linked rooms, was full of spies and hundreds of people coming and going who could listen in on a conversation. As the saying goes, the walls had ears, but Nell's house was secure and a safe haven.

There were magnificent celebrations on 29 May for Charles' fortieth birthday and also the tenth year of his restoration. He spent the day with his sister and celebrated with a royal banquet at sea. Although Nell could not attend the court festivities in honour of the King's sister due to her humble background, it was said that Minette was well aware of her brother's mistress and the new baby and she sent gifts to Nell of 'boxes of perfumed gloves, little mirrors, apricot paste and the other small wares of love.'[3]

Too soon, it was Minette's time to return to France. Charles showered her with gifts and asked that she leave him a jewel of her own. When Louise Renée de Penancoët de Kérouaille was ushered into the chamber with a casket from which Charles was to choose a token, he told Minette that she (Louise) was the jewel he most coveted. His sister was well aware of her brother's tastes but Louise needed to return to France – for now.

As the King waved farewell to his sister, he didn't know it would be the last time he saw her. Not long after her return to France she died, some thought of poisoning, given to her by her husband, or his lover, the Chevalier de Lorraine. Charles was bereft. Buckingham was sent to France to represent the King at Minette's funeral while Charles stayed at Whitehall to be comforted by the Queen, and, in the evenings, by Nell.

The couple escaped to Newmarket for a break and Nell helped to soothe away the King's pain and grief. Evelyn saw the King's new house being built but was not so happy with its situation, 'this house is place in a dirty street without any court or avenue like a common one, whereas it might and ought to have been built at either end of the town, upon the very carpet where the sports are celebrated; but, it being the purchase of an old wretched house of my Lord Thomond's, his Majesty was persuaded to set it on that foundation, the most improper imaginable for a house of sport and pleasure.'[4] But it was close to Nell's and that was more important.

Barbara's star was falling even further after the King caught her in bed with John Churchill who abruptly left through a window. Charles refused to acknowledge any more of her children. It was obvious she had many lovers and these days he could not be sure who she was sleeping with. He forgave Churchill, saying, 'I forgive you, for you only do it for your bread,' but if he ever had any control over Barbara, and that is debatable, their relationship was souring now.

In August 1670 Barbara was given the title of Duchess of Cleveland as well as Countess of Southampton and Baroness Nonsuch since Charles had already granted her Henry VIII's former royal palace. Henry VIII had died before the palace was completed and in Mary I's reign it was sold to Henry FitzAlan, 19th Earl of Arundel, who completed it before it was returned to the crown in the 1590s. It changed hands again after the English Civil War, when it was given to General Thomas Pride. He died in 1658 and after Charles was restored to the throne, it once again became royal property. The king never used it and chose to gift it to Barbara but it would be the end of the palace as she had it stripped down, dismantled and sold. The ever-grasping Barbara had the last laugh as her relationship with the King ended with her receiving a title and a pension of £30,000 a year.

Nell could say goodbye to one of her rivals at long last, but with Charles' sister's death, that jewel he had so admired, Louise de Kérouaille was out of a job and preparing to travel to England. This young woman was from a noble but poor family from Brittany. She had a convent education before becoming one of Minette's ladies and had grown up at the French court. After Minette's funeral, Buckingham mentioned to King Louis that Louise, with her curly dark hair and brown eyes, might serve both courts well if she were to be given a position at the English court. Ever scheming, Buckingham saw it as another way to usurp the Queen. It was agreed that Louise could become one of Catherine's maids of honour and he felt sure she would rise in the King's affections. But first she had to get to England. Buckingham lent her his carriage to take her to Dieppe but took sail without his new charge. Louise was left stranded and furious at the duke, a slight she would never forgive. She had to wait until Lord Arlington sent a boat and servants to accompany her to Whitehall.

Although Louise was welcomed at court and was a great comfort to the King, sharing with him stories of his sister's life in France to assuage his grief, he would not yet begin the chase for her affections. She came with the grace and manners of the French court and brought with her new fashions and styles that appealed to the ladies. Where once the Queen had been laughed at for her old-fashioned ways, Louise was modern and refreshing and it made her popular – at least for a time. In her apartments at Whitehall they flocked to see her, including the French ambassador and other French exiles. They recognised how close to power she would become.

We don't know when Louise and Nell first met but Nell disliked her and her pompous ways from the start, giving her the nicknames of 'weeping willow' and 'squintabella'. This French woman was a threat to her position as mistress and her popularity put Nell's nose out of joint. She had an ally in Buckingham, who had tried to win Louise over after leaving her stranded, but she would not tolerate him and he had no time for her. The two of them devised a skit for the amusement of Nell's dinner party guests where Buckingham, as Charles, showered Nell, as Louise, with jewels, but she sobbed and wailed, declaring in a French accent: 'me no bad woman. If me taut me was one bad woman, me would cut mine own trote.'[5]

Some people, including Lord Arlington, Secretary of State, were more than happy to see Charles with a new mistress. The French ambassador reported: 'My Lord Arlington told me recently that he was very glad to see the King his master attached to her (Louise), for although His Majesty never communicated state affairs to ladies, nevertheless as they could on occasion injure those whom they hate and in that way ruin business, it was better for all good servants of the King that his attraction should be to Mademoiselle Keroualle, whose humour was not mischievous and who was a lady, rather than to lewd and bouncing orange-girls and actresses, of whom no honest man could take the measure.'[6]

In December 1670 Nell returned to stage in the first part of *The Conquest of Granada* as Almahide, Queen of the Moors. Dryden had written the part especially for her. She practiced her role in front of Charles, dressing in character. Once on the stage, she performed the part wearing a hat the size of a cartwheel. Since Louise was alluded to in the play and her surname was difficult to pronounce, 'Cartwheel' became just the name for her. Nell would call her far worse but behind closed doors.

The play ended with Dryden's nod to Nell's year off while she had her son:

> Think him not duller for this year's delay;
> He was prepared, the women were away;
> And men, without their parts, can hardly play.
> If they, through sickness, seldom did appear,
> Pity the virgins of each theatre:
> For at both houses 'twas a sickly year!
> And pity us, your servants, to whose cost,
> In one such sickness, nine whole months are lost.[7]

Charles' infatuation with women was general gossip but it sometimes took a sinister turn. On 21 December 1670 Nell's friend Sir Thomas Sandys and some others attacked Sir John Coventry for poking fun at the King's lovers in the House of Commons. During a debate on whether to tax the playhouses, Coventry had asked 'whether did the king's pleasure lie among the men or the women that acted?' – a pointed reference to Nell and Moll. The King's friends and Nell's supporters were incensed and Coventry was later set upon, trussed up in a blanket and his nose slit to the bone, some said on the Duke of Monmouth's orders.

The outcry that followed resulted in the passing of a law called the Coventry Act, which stated: 'that if any person shall of malice aforethought, and by lying in wait, unlawfully cut out or disable the tongue, put out an eye, slit the nose, cut off a nose or lip, or cut off or disable any limb or member of any other person, with intent to main or disfigure him; such person, his counselors, aiders, and abettors, shall be guilty of a capital felony without the benefit of clergy.'[8]

But some pointed the finger at Nell. A ballad 'The Haymarket Hectors' ran:

> Our good King Charles the Second, too flippant of treasure
>   and moisture,
> Stooped from the Queen infecund to a wench of orange and
>   oyster;
> Consulting his Catzo, he found it expedient
> To waste his time in revels with Nell the comedian.
>
> Oye Hay-Market Hector, how cam you thus charmed,
> To be dissectors of one poor Nose unarmed?
> Unfit to wear a sword, or follow a trumpet,
> That would brandish your knives at the word of a strumpet?
>
> If the sister of Rose be a whore so anointed
> That the Parliament's Nose for her be disjointed,
> Then should you but name the prerogative whore,
> How the bullets would whistle, the cannons would roar[9]

Nell, of course, had no part in Coventry's beating but her friend Sandys spent some time in prison for the assault. She visited his wife, Lucy – another lady who would become a lifelong friend – while he was incarcerated.

A fire at the playhouse in January 1671 meant there was no work for the time being, except for entertaining the King and he was planning a grand ballet. In February 1671 the ballet was held at Whitehall to mark the end of the mourning period for Minette. The Queen, Frances and Louise, with the Duchesses of Monmouth and Buckingham, led the dances. Crowds gathered at the palace from as early as 4pm for the evening performance but there was no sign of Nell. 'After the ballet was over several others danced, as the Duke of York, and the King, and the Duke of Buckingham. And the Duchess of Cleveland was very fine in a rich petticoat and halfe shirte and a short man's coat very richly laced, a periwig, cravat and hat.'[10] Nell was not invited; her position not suitably raised to attend with the other ladies. It must have stung.

Nell had her own personal triumph though – a beautiful new home at 79 Pall Mall, a much grander townhouse than her previous property. She moved there in February 1671 with plans for its decoration. She had a deadline for May as she wanted to make sure it was looking fabulous for the King's upcoming birthday. Her reception room was dazzling and the talk of the town with mirrors that covered the walls from floor to ceiling.

Nell came into her own with her new property, a testament to her new status. It was her perfect home and filled with the hustle and bustle of servants she treated as family. She had Thomas Groundes as her steward for managing her day-to-day business and accounts, James Booth as her secretary, and a lady's maid, Bridget Long, to take her letters, as well as other staff, including a coachman, footmen, a cook, kitchen maids, chambermaids, washerwomen and pages. She would also have had nursemaids for her sons. Male servants all wore her livery although unfortunately nothing remains to tell us what colours she chose or what badges they wore. Nell had come a long way from the dirty back alleys of London and a hand-to-mouth existence. She was a lady now, in everything but name.

A ribald verse commemorated her move both to a new home and a more steady footing with Charles:

> Hard by Pall Mall lives a wench name'd Nell,
> King Charlie the Second he kept her.
> She hath a trick to handle his prick,
> But she'll never lay hands on his scepter!
> All matters of state from her soul she does hate,
> And leave to the politic bitches.
> The whore's in the right, for 'tis her delight
> To be scratching just where it itches.[11]

Of course the King would be a regular visitor. Their relationship was flourishing – never mind Louise – and Nell knew he adored her. Never mind the other mistresses, Nell had the man she loved, a child she adored and a house she could never have dreamed of. Despite what other people thought, she was content.

The diarist Evelyn, however, was ashamed at seeing Nell and the King together in March: 'I thence walked … through St James's Park to the garden, where I both saw and heard a familiar discourse between … and Mrs Nelly, as they called an impudent comedian, she looking out of her garden on a terrace at the top of the wall and … standing on the green walk under it. I was heartily sorry at this scene. Thence the King walked to the Duchess of Cleveland, another lady of pleasure, and curse of our nation.'[12]

Did Nell know that after talking to her he went on to see Barbara? Would she even have cared? By this time Charles' visits to Barbara were mostly to see their children at Berkshire House, now named Cleveland House after her new title. Barbara had other lovers including William Wycherley, the playwright. She was no longer a rival for the King's affection. She had got what she wanted and moved on. Nell was secure as she could be in her new house and she was expecting her second child. When Nell had first caught the King's eye Barbara had been friendly towards her, but their relationship had soured. Barbara made real enemies and was hated by many who saw her as a complete drain on the Crown and a political agitator. Nell just laughed at the woman, and as with all of the King's mistresses, she didn't pass up an opportunity to send her up. When Barbara got a new coach and six horses, the story goes that Nell hired a cart and six oxen to drive past Cleveland House shouting 'Whores to market, Ho!'

With preparations made for the King's birthday party, Buckingham tried to wrangle an invitation for his mistress, Anna Maria Brudenell, Countess of Shrewsbury, whose husband Buckingham had killed in a duel in January 1668. Charles passed on the message but Nell was having none of it, telling him that 'one whore at a time was enough for his Majesty.'[13] Buckingham's wife had also been unimpressed when he turned up with his mistress in tow at the family home in Wallingford. When the duchess told him it was not done for them all to live together, he told her to get the coach and horses ready to take her to her father's.

That summer was spent at Windsor. Nell lodged in a house on Church Street. It was rumoured there was a secret tunnel to the King's bedchamber from hers for their night-time trysts – a rumour that is probably attached to every house Nell stayed in! Charles, of course, stayed at the castle, which needed improving since its dereliction during the Interregnum. '[The] King's house was a wreck; the fanatic, the pilferer, and the squatter, having been at work ... Paupers had squatted in many of the towers and cabinets.'[14] Repairs were underway and Charles would commission a new suite of state apartments and the rebuilding of the castle's defences.

Prince Rupert of the Rhine, who was made Constable of the Tower, was there to oversee the work with his mistress, another former actress, Peg Hughes. Peg, once the mistress of Sir Charles Sedley, had met Prince Rupert at Tunbridge Wells in 1668. Nell immediately took to the prince and joined them for dinner and evening entertainment. Many evenings were spent with friends and late nights of drinking and partying meant Nell often slept the whole morning away. Afternoons were for country pursuits and Nell would often accompany the King to Datchet to fish – a new interest for Charles.

Louise spent the summer at Whitehall saying she did not like the countryside. When the court moved to Newmarket, Nell went to her little house there built by Christopher Wren, and Louise, probably realising that if she didn't step up she would lose the King, stayed nearby as a guest at Euston Hall, the country seat of Lord Arlington. Evelyn noted in his diary: 'It was universally reported that the fair lady – was bedded one of these nights, and the stocking flung, after the manner of a married bride; I acknowledge she was for the most part in her undress all day, and that there was fondness and toying with that young wanton, nay, it was said I was at the former ceremony, but it is utterly false ... However, it was with confidence believed she was made a Miss, as they call these unhappy creatures, with solemnity at this time.'[15]

A mock wedding had taken place, as Barbara had once done with Frances Stuart. Perhaps it was this pretend marriage that gave Louise notions as she held the belief that one day she would not just be the King's mistress but his Queen. The French ambassador Croissy reported she was making an utter fool of herself, 'because she does not keep her head sober, since she has got the notion into it that it is possible she may yet be Queen of England. She talks from morning to night of the Queen's ailments as if they were mortal.'[16] Louise was just waiting for the current Queen to die in the expectation that Charles would marry her.

Nell was seven months pregnant at the time and thought the King deserved a small comeuppance for Louise's bedding. She knew she could not do anything too drastic as it would only anger him and jeopardise their relationship. She may have disliked Louise intently but the King could not be faithful. Playing on this, she got Buckingham to help her with a prank. He was to take Charles to a brothel with some of their friends for a bawdy night out, and while he was having his pleasure, they took his money and fled leaving him alone and penniless. The constable was called out to do something about this non-paying customer and Charles had to prove who he was by showing them his coronation ring, mortified he had been caught out.

Although Louise was initially popular people soon tired of her. She was rightly rumoured to be a French spy, and a Catholic one at that, and after her bedding by her 'Chanticleer' her attitude became more and more insufferable. Nell had her measure. Madame de Sevigne wrote of Nell's attitude: 'As to (Nell) she reasons thus: this duchess, says she, pretends to be a person of quality. If she be a lady of such quality, why does she demean herself to be a whore? She ought to die for shame. As for me, it is my profession: I do not pretend to be anything better.'[17]

Nell, however, was still loved by the people and she was Charles' link to them as 'Nell's little hand in the king's was the hand of his people.'[18] She told him of the real world beyond Whitehall and the real lives of the people who were his subjects. The general public, so sick of the King's mistresses who flaunted their wealth, still loved that a woman of such low birth had risen so far. For Nell's part, Charles was everything to her. Would he have been if he were not King? We shall never know, but in Nell, Charles had a loyal companion and in return she gave him joy and mirth and evenings of pleasure. She was the least demanding of his mistresses and the most loyal. Louise would do her best to make Charles give up his little actress, even complaining 'anybody may know she has been an orange girl by her swearing,'[19] but the King would never forsake his Nelly.

Nell gave birth to a second son who was christened James after the Duke of York, on Christmas Day 1671 in the cold of winter, but his birth sent the rumour mill into overdrive. Gossips claimed Nell had been given £20,000 for providing the King with another son. It generated a tale of how Barbara and Louise plotted to do away with their rival by inviting her to dinner, getting her drunk and then choking her to death, but when people saw Nell out and about they realised it was just another rumour surrounding the King's mistresses.

There was another fire at the King's Playhouse on 25 January 1672 and this time Nell was horrified to hear there was a fatality. 'A fire at the King's play house between 7-8 on Thursday evening last, which half burned down the house and all their scenes and wardrobe; and all the houses from the Rose Tavern on Russell Street on that side of the way to Drury lane are burned and blown up, with many in Vinegar yard; £20,000 damage. The fire began under the stairs where Orange Moll keeps her fruit. Bell the Player was blown up.'[20]

Killigrew, who often visited Nell, told her that at this point they were looking to build a new playhouse. Nell must have been sorry that it had come to this but she would no longer grace the stage, old or new. There are some accounts of Nell's appearances on the stage after 1671, as in Beaumont and Fletcher's *A King and No King*, but she did not take on any new roles. Instead she would visit and watch her old comrades acting in the latest plays, and if she felt like entertaining she could dress up for the King at one of her parties. Charles was a generous master, but not so much for Nell as he had been with others. Still, he helped out her sister, Rose, with a yearly pension and a pardon for her errant husband, Cassells, who had burgled Sir Henry Littleton's house. There was more than one perk to being the King's lover.

But she also had to soothe a troubled Charles in times of unrest. On 7 June 1672 the Battle of Solebay, near Southwold in Suffolk, took place. It was the first naval battle of the third Anglo-Dutch War, a direct result of the secret treaty of Dover. English ships under the command of the Duke of York as Lord Admiral and the Earl of Sandwich joined with French vessels to attack the Dutch fleet. People stood in their hundreds along the coast to watch the battle and made ready should England fall and the Dutch invade. The fight raged all day with no clear winner. Both sides lost two ships and around 2,000 men – the English casualties including the Earl of Sandwich. Charles rushed to meet his brother once he was back on shore. Nell felt his relief after days of worry but there was shock and dismay at the vice-admiral's death. Sandwich's ship had been blown to smithereens. His burnt body washed ashore and was only recognised by his clothing. Sandwich met Evelyn before he left for war and the diarist recalled, 'he bid me good-by, and said he thought he would see me no more, and I saw, to my thinking, something boding in his countenance.'[21] Sadly he was right.

There were more joyous occasions in the summer. Barbara gave birth to a baby girl in July, but it was probably not the King's, she having moved on to other lovers. Charles, however, did acknowledge the child, named Barbara Fitzroy, but it would be the last of the Duchess of Cleveland's children he would recognise. And Louise de Kérouaille also gave birth to Charles II's last son in July, a boy they called Charles – yet another one named after his father. The King now had at least twelve illegitimate children. Moll Davis, as mentioned before, gave birth to the King's daughter, Mary Tudor, and the date most commonly given is the following year, 1673. We know nothing of Moll's life during these years so it is possible that he still visited her on occasion, but the King, often suffering from syphilis and the inevitable treatment of large doses of mercury, wasn't quite the womaniser that he used to be.

Nell was back in fine form after having her son and while Louise was still recovering from the birth of hers – and upset that the King had not yet acknowledged their son – Nell spent more time with Charles. Buckingham, however, must have thought his relationship with Nell was far closer than it was. Thinking he was in with a chance, he tried to get more familiar with her in the King's apartments, receiving a resounding smack in the face for his trouble. Little Nell was not about to jeopardise her relationship with the King regardless of who his current paramour was. The Venetian ambassador reported: 'Buckingham is now in disgrace with the King for an audacious attempt on His Majesty's private pleasures.'[22] While the King's other mistresses may take lovers or husbands, Nell would always stay true to her King.

Chapter Five

The Mistresses Govern All 1673-1675

BACK in 1672 the King announced the Royal Declaration of Indulgence to promote religious tolerance. As per the secret Treaty of Dover, he was aiming to take steps towards making England a Catholic country, but he made no attempt to change his own faith, knowing that there would be a public outcry. His mother, Queen Henrietta Maria, had been Catholic, and the Duke of York, his brother, had converted in 1668, but we can't be sure whether at this stage Charles really wanted to join them.

Following on from the declaration of 1672, the next year saw a complete turnaround and the Test Act, or 'An act for preventing dangers which may happen from popish recusants', came into force, which meant that Catholics were not allowed in positions of power and were banned from public service. An oath had to be taken: 'I, (name) do declare that I do believe that there is not any transubstantiation in the sacrament of the Lord's Supper, or in the elements of the bread and wine, at or after the consecration thereof by any person whatsoever.'[1]

The Duke of York had to resign his command of the fleet as Lord High Admiral and Prince Rupert, the King's nephew, took over. The 'cabal', the King's private council, made up of Thomas Clifford, 1st Baron Clifford of Chudleigh, Anthony Ashley-Cooper, 1st Earl of Shaftesbury, George Villiers, 2nd Duke of Buckingham, Henry Bennet, 1st Earl of Arlington and John Maitland, 1st Duke of Lauderdale, ended too. Clifford resigned as treasurer, later committing suicide, and Thomas Osborne, later the Earl of Danby, took his place. Danby would be no friend to Nell. For the moment it did not worry her although her relationship with Danby would soon sour.

Everyone knew Nell was a Protestant and attended services at her family's church at St Martin-in-the-Fields, unlike the King's wife and other mistresses. Queen Catherine's household was reduced to only nine Catholic ladies being allowed in her employ. Barbara had converted to Catholicism back in December 1663. At the time her family had been greatly shocked and asked the King to do something about it, but his response was 'as for the souls of ladies, he never meddled with that.'[2] Now it meant she lost her position as Lady of the Bedchamber.

Louise, high in the King's favour, kept her place and on 5 July 1673 Nell's nemesis was created Duchess of Portsmouth, Countess of Farnham and Baroness Petersfield, and she threw a lavish ball at Barn Elms to celebrate. Nell was furious. It may have been asking too much but she had hoped to be given a title herself. She thought perhaps 'Countess of Plymouth' would suit and discussed it with Charles, who gave her some hope. She even 'got a patent drawne to bee Countess of Plymouth but ye Lord Keeper refused to seale itt before hee first spoak with ye King who told him, hee was but in iest with her.'[3] Her background meant that she would never really be a candidate for ennoblement, or as Chesterton, one of her biographers, put it, 'To have made the orange-girl a peeress would have been an affront to something much stronger than the moral sentiment of the middle classes; it would have been an affront to the idea of aristocracy.'[4]

Louise didn't only get a title but her sister, Henrietta Mauricette, also received a dowry and pension. The King's French mistress had asked if her sister could be made welcome at court and Charles sent a boat for the woman who the Marquis de Ruvigny derogatively said was 'nothing to look at.'[5] A marriage was duly arranged for her with Philip Herbert, the 5th Earl of Pembroke, and after their wedding they went to live at his home, Wilton House in Wiltshire, where the abuse began. Pembroke was a strange choice for a husband. He was a violent drunk and had been involved in several assaults, but worse was to come. In time he would commit several murders.

Louise's sister fled back to Whitehall until she could safely return to France. Pembroke hated Louise and her interference, swearing he would turn her on her head so that the people could see just what the King saw in her. Nell would have loved to see it. It hurt to have someone she loathed raised to the peerage, and by her own lover. Charles had given Louise everything, including her own apartments at Whitehall which she decorated in the French style. The bills, of course, were footed by the King.

Evelyn gave a glorious description when he visited his majesty:

> I went, with the few who attended him, into the Duchess of
> Portsmouth's dressing room within her bed-chamber, where
> she was in her morning loose garment, her maids combing
> her, newly out of her bed, his Majesty and the gallants
> standing about her; but that which engaged my curiosity was
> the rich and splendid furniture of this woman's apartment,
> now twice or thrice pulled down and rebuilt to satisfy her
> prodigal and expensive pleasures, whilst her Majesty's
> does not exceed some gentlemen's ladies in furniture and
> accommodation. Here I saw the new fabric of French
> tapestry, for design, tenderness of work, and incomparable
> imitation of the best paintings, beyond anything I had ever
> beheld. Some pieces had Versailles, St Germain's, and
> other palaces of the French King, with huntings, figures,
> and landscapes, exotic fowls, and all to the life rarely don.
> Then Japan cabinets, screens, pendula clocks, great vases
> of wrought plate, tables, stands, chimney furniture, sconces,
> branches, braseras, &c. all of massive silver, and out of
> number, besides some of her Majesty's best paintings[6]

Charles also ordered an expensive silver dinner service be made for
his mistress and it was put on display in the silversmith's shop window.
Londoners ogled the luxurious plate but the more vicious whispered it
should be melted down and poured down her throat. Others felt 'it was
a thousand pities His Majesty had not bestowed this bounty on Madam
Ellen.'[7] Nell, not to be outdone, bought her own solid silver service
engraved with her initials – E.G.

However, Nell was not doing too badly herself. She loved her house
in Pall Mall and filled it full of beautiful things. She had a magnificent
silver bed, commissioned from John Coques, for her tumbles with the
King. It was a stunning piece of bedroom furniture and Nell made sure
the imagery around the bed resonated with her mischievous nature.
There was the King's head and coronet to represent Charles. Her sons
appeared as cherubs – all symbolising her family. Then there was the
figure of Jacob Hall, the rope-dancer, balancing on a wire – a nod to
Barbara who had taken him as a lover – and Louise appeared, lying in a

tomb with an Eastern potentate. The silversmith was asked not only to make it but to organise the cleaning and repair of other household items.

Some items on the silversmith's bill show Nell was not doing too badly and included:

Delivered the head of ye bedstead weighing 885 ounces 12lb.

Delivered ye kings head weighing 197oz 5dwt

ye two Eagles weighing 169oz 10dwt

one of the crowns weighing 94oz 5dwt

Paid for Jacob Hall dancing upon ye rope of wire-work £1 10 0d.

For ye cleansing and burnishing a sugar box, a pepper box, a mustard pot, and two kruyzes £0 12s. 0d.

Paid to ye cabinet-maker for ye greatte board for ye head of the bedstead and for ye other board that comes under it and boring the holes into ye (bedstead) head £3 0s. 0d.

Paid to Mr Consar for carving ye said board £10 0s. 0d.

For ye bettering ye solder wich was in the old bedstead £5 3s. 7d.

Paid to ye smith for ye ironwork to hold up ye Eagles and for ye two hooks to hold the bedstead against the wall £0 3s. 0d.

Paid for ye pedestal of ebony to hold up the 2 georses £1 10s. 0d.

For ye mending of y gold hourglass £0 2s. 6d.

For ye cleansing of eight pictures £0 10s. 0d.

In all comes to £1135 3s. 1d.[8]

The bill came to around £100,000 in today's money. The remodelling of Nell's bedroom to be the most sumptuous room in the house involved the work of carvers, smiths and cabinet makers to make items such as a silver looking glass decorated with images of the King and Nell, two wainscot seats with compass ends engraved with the initials CR and NG and an upholsterer to make sky-blue satin curtains. The entire remodelling would not be finished till August 1675.

Moll Davis had also moved to a new house, a handsome three-storey building on the south-west side of St James's Square. Her daughter by the King was supposedly born in October this year. If so, it meant that Charles was still visiting the former actress. The King liked rewarding his mistresses after the birth of their children, although there is no record he footed the bill and Moll bought the property from trustees for Edward Shaw, paying £1,800. That Moll was so well off is strange in itself. She was living way above her £1,000 a year pension from the King and would not marry until later in life yet she must have found a wealthy patron, if not Charles himself.

In February 1674 England and the Dutch Republic signed the Treaty of Westminster which ended the Third Anglo-Dutch War. The King no longer had the support of Parliament or the funds to keep it going. England would be at peace for the rest of Charles' reign. He had more time to spend with his darling Nelly and she kept him royally entertained with her charm and wit, inviting entertaining guests to her superb supper parties. In quiet times together they discussed the news of the day and there was also a startling discovery by workmen at the Tower of London when two skeletons were found.

John Knight, the King's surgeon, recorded:

> In order to the rebuilding of several Offices in the Tower, and to clear the White Tower from all contiguous building, digging down the stairs which led from the King's Lodgings, to the Chapel in the said Tower, about ten foot in the ground were found the Bones of two striplings in (as it seemed) a wooden chest, which upon the survey were found proportionable to the ages of those two Brothers viz. about thirteen and eleven years. The skull of the one being entire, the other broken, as were indeed many of the other Bones, also the chest, by the violence of the laborers, who cast the rubbish and them away together, wherefore they were caused to sift the rubbish, and by that means preserved all the bones. The circumstances being often discoursed with Sir Thomas Chichley, Master of the Ordinance, by whose

industry the new Buildings were then in carrying on, and by
whom this matter was reported to the King.[9]

The story of the princes in the Tower had passed down through the
years and it was believed that their remains had finally been found.
Charles would later have them buried in Westminster Abbey in a marble
urn designed by Christopher Wren which includes the inscription,
'Charles II, a most compassionate prince, pitying their severe fate,
ordered these unhappy Princes to be laid amongst the monuments of
their predecessors'.

In the same year the King's Playhouse reopened, on 26 March, and Nell
was given her own box. There was another woman who had successfully
switched from orange girl to actress. Betty Mackerel, or 'Orange Betty',
would join the company that year and Nell was eager to see how she
performed. She also visited their rival theatre: between September 1674
and June 1676 Nell would go to the Duke's Playhouse at Dorset Gardens
fifty-five times. She saw *The Tempest or The Enchanted Island,* William
Davenant's adaptation of Shakespeare's comedy *The Tempest*, no fewer than
four times in the autumn of 1674, clearly enjoying the extravagant musical
comedy, with special effects including a shower of fire and an aerial ballet.
She may not have been on the stage any more, although playwrights would
continue to dedicate their plays to her in the hope she might return, but she
still spent many hours at the theatre, often with the King.

The Queen had once complained that 'the mistresses govern all',[10]
but one of them was about to pay for her indiscretions. At the end of
1674 Louise was unfortunate enough to catch the 'French pox', or
syphilis, from Charles. She would be ill for nearly a year and went from
spa to spa in search of a treatment. The King of France sent her gifts of
pearls and diamonds in a bid to cheer her up, and she needed cheering up;
apart from her illness, she was depressed because of her unpopularity.
It was becoming more apparent how much she was resented, and not just
by the common people, but the nobility too.

She had had an unhappy encounter in the summer when she wanted
rooms at Tunbridge Wells but found that Lady Worcester had taken them.
She ordered her to vacate them and expected her wishes to be carried
out, she was the King's mistress after all but Lady Worcester was having
none of it. 'The marchioness told her she had better blood in her veins
than e'er a French bitch in the world and that the English nobility would

not be affronted by her, calling her tall bitch. There might you have seen their towers (headdresses) and hair flying about the room, as the miserable spoils of so fierce an encounter. The Marchioness beat her upon the face, got her down and kicked her, and finally forced her out of doors.'[11]

This may well be exaggerated as Lady Worcester would surely have been reprimanded for such a physical altercation although Charles was wont to not interfere in the ladies squabbles. With his amount of mistresses and a queen to juggle, he found it best not to play referee when it came to their disagreements although he did try at times to get Nell and Louise to endure each other. On one occasion, when the three were at dinner, Louise tried and failed to be witty by telling the king she had three pieces of chicken on her plate when there was only two. 'How so?' asked Charles and the giggling Louise said 'One piece, two piece; and one and two piece makes three pieces!' Nell, never to be outdone leant over and took the chicken off her plate saying 'If that's the case, then I'll have one piece, Charles can have one piece, and you can have the third piece for yourself!'

How Nell was never affected by syphilis – not that we know of – remains a mystery. Perhaps she suffered in silence, but given the rumour mill at the time, we would surely know if she had been ill. It is possible, though, that she had early symptoms and these then left her for years, returning to affect her health later in life.

Although there was no cure at the time, her mother, perhaps, had passed on tricks of the trade. There were plenty of remedies, the most reputed being mercury. As the saying went, 'A night with Venus, a lifetime with Mercury,' though this cure caused more problems than it solved. Nicholas Culpeper, the infamous herbalist, recommended the use of heartsease (wild pansy) and physicians advised purging, bleeding and various treatments, but, of course, none of these worked. Condoms were sometimes used by the nobility, more to stop pregnancy than to prevent sexual disease. These were made from animal bladders and tied with a ribbon to 'receive all without hazard' although it's unlikely that the King ever used them.

*****

Nell was known for her smart remarks and put downs. She never missed an opportunity to get her own back on those who lorded over her. Courtin, the French ambassador, described her as 'the frisking comedian'[12] and Louise de Keroualle was one of her favourite targets. In December 1674 word reached the court of the death of the Chevalier de Rohan and Louise made a show of herself, weeping and wailing at the loss of her supposed distant relation while dressed in the finest mourning clothes. Charles grew exasperated and had her escorted back to her rooms. He had no time for her hysterics.

When Nell heard about Louise's behaviour, she thought it a perfect way to send her up and the next day appeared in her own mourning clothes, devastated at the death of her made-up Cham of Tartary. Using all of her acting skills, she put on a performance like no other, gleefully laughing at the stuck-up Louise. When asked who the Cham was and what relation he was to Nell, she is reported to have said, 'he was as close to me as the Chevalier de Rohan was to the Duchess of Portsmouth.'[13] When the King of Sweden died and Louise once more donned her mourning garb, Nell remarked, 'Let us settle this matter. We shall divide the world. You shall have the Kings of the North and I shall have those of the South.'[14]

On another occasion, Nell saw Louise on her way to see the King and the French mistress commented that Nell had such beautiful clothes, she could be a Queen. To which Nell replied, 'And you, Cartwheel, look whore enough to be a duchess.'[15]

Louise was a constant thorn in Nell's side. In her role as a lady of the bedchamber, Louise waited on the Queen. When Catherine of Braganza became ill, Louise hovered over her, awaiting her chance to be Charles' next wife. The Queen was wise to her husband's mistress and told her she was 'at the wrong monarch's pillow.'[16] Louise talked constantly of how ill the Queen was and everyone knew her ambition, but Nell was not concerned. She knew 'the nation will never have her.'[17]

Madame de Sévigné would later sum up the relationship between the two in a letter to her daughter, although she clearly was no fan of Nell's.

> Mademoiselle de Keroualle has been disappointed in nothing; she wished to be the mistress of the King, and she is so ... She amasses treasure, and makes herself feared and respected as much a she can. But she did not foresee that she should find a young actress in her way, whom the King dotes on; and she has not it in her power to withdraw him from her. He divides his care, his time and

his health between these two. The actress is as haughty as the Duchess of Portsmouth; she insults her, makes faces at her, attacks her, frequently steals the King from her, and boasts of his preference for her. She is young, indiscreet, confident, meretricious and pleasant; she sings, dances, and acts her part well. She has a son by the King, and wishes to have him acknowledged: she reasons thus: "This Duchess," says she, "pretends to be a person of quality; she says she is related to the best families in France; whenever any person of consequence dies, she puts herself in mourning. If she be a lady of such quality why does she demean herself to be a courtesan? She ought to be ashamed of herself. As for me, it is my profession; I do not pretend to be anything better. The King maintains me, and I am constant to him at present. He has a son by me: I say he ought to acknowledge him, and I am sure he will for he loves me as well as he does Portsmouth." This creature gets the upper hand, and discountenances and embarrasses the Duchess extremely.[18]

Sometimes the pair of them had get along to appease the King and on occasion they were friendly, sharing tea or playing cards. All of the King's mistresses, even the Queen, had to accept each another. Charles was their focus and they were merely satellites to his star: if the King was unhappy, they all would feel the effects. But Nell could never pass up a chance to best her rival.

Nell had many portraits painted, mainly by Peter Lely, Simon Verelst and Henri Gascar. When Gascar arrived at court in 1674, Louise was one of the first to be painted by him. The portrait is now on display at Castle Coole in Northern Ireland. In it, the duchess is depicted as Venus, sitting reclining on cushions wearing a lace-trimmed red and white satin chemise, one breast exposed, holding a dove. St James's Park can be seen in the background. Nell, with mischief on her mind, had a fellow conspirator steal the chemise and had her own portrait painted by Gascar. She was portrayed as a more alluring Venus, suggestively lying back on a bed of flowers, both breasts exposed and her sons as Cupids flying towards her. The background of St James's Park is the same, except in this portrait the King stands watching her. Nell made sure it took pride of place in her home at Pall Mall. She would not be outdone by Squintabella!

Lely would become a friend of Nell's and often visited her house in Pall Mall. She loved the way he painted her nearly naked or exposing a breast. In one portrait, possibly of Nell (although debated), she is dressed as a shepherdess, one hand draped over a lamb and her bare breasts exposed. In fact, nearly all of Nell's portraits showed her cleavage. Verelyst, a Dutch painter, painted her with rosy red cheeks, both breasts bare and her skin a milky white. The miniaturist Peter Cross, who would become Charles' limner-in-ordinary, also depicted Nell naked with angel's wings, holding cupid's dart.

Lely, Charles II's Principal Painter in Ordinary, had risen to become one of the greatest court painters, so popular in fact that he had a team of assistants who painted in backgrounds and dresses while he concentrated on the face and hands. At his studio in Drury Lane, he welcomed Nell for another of her most popular portraits, that of her and her son. She was Venus again, he Cupid. All she wore was a tiny white slip of cloth across her lap. While Lely was painting, Charles would visit and 'when she was naked on purpose'[19] watch his mistress reveal herself in all her glory. Nell loved the painting so much she had it in pride of place in her mirror-lined reception hall. That way if Charles' eyes strayed to anyone else, her picture was a reminder of her assets. The King had his copy in Whitehall (years later Buckingham would take it down and keep it for himself).

When Nell did have on clothes she loved to dress well and had her favourite dressmakers, George Hookett and Humphrey Dutton. They made her petticoats, her red satin nightdresses, white hose, pink and white coats and beautiful lace-trimmed dresses. Nell ordered materials by the armful: satin, lace, damask, scotch cloth, Holland and paragon made from Angora goat's wool in a variety of colours. Her sister, Rose also helped with alterations and sourcing supplies. One time, Rose lamented, writing to Nell, 'I have sent you the rest of the ribbon and lace that was left. I was in twenty shops looking for cheaper but could not (find any) for my life.'[20] Pretty shoes showed off one of her finest assets to their great advantage and she ordered them in abundance: satin with gold lace, scarlet shoes richly laced, green satin shoes with gold and silver chain, pink satin slippers and sky coloured shoes – not to mention those she bought for her children.

She loved her jewellery, especially pearls, and wore them for her portraits. And, as many women did who could afford it, she wore rings, necklaces and hairpins, all adorned with diamonds and pearls and was particularly fond of a gold locket that contained a miniature of Charles, painted by Peter Cross for £23 9s. Interestingly, a necklace she would later buy from Peg Hughes, Prince Rupert's mistress, appears in one of her portraits, but she must have just borrowed it for the painting. Jewellery was quite typically loaned for special occasions. And, of course, her hair had to be just right for her portraits. She followed the current trend of an 'abundance of curles very small on their heads, and very fine their heads dressed.'[21] Often there would be pearls in her up-do and she paid a good deal for her coronets and coifs. Spending money on clothes, jewellery, shoes and her hair was important and not just frivolous expenditure as Nell had an image to maintain in public and in private. She was noticed wherever she went and she had a King to look good for.

Louise also spent a fortune on herself, but she and Nell were worlds apart in their outlook on life. Whereas Louise expected everything, Nell expected nothing and was all the more grateful for what she received, and where Louise took things to heart, Nell shrugged them off, rolling with the punches and usually coming up trumps.

One day Louise was held up by 'old Mobb', a notorious highwayman, as she travelled in her coach out of London. Her haughty reaction was to ask him if he knew who she was. He did indeed and replied, 'I know you to be the greatest whore in the kingdom and that you are maintained at the public charge.'[22] He continued to say he didn't care for her Frenchness but her English coin was good. Louise was shocked and left by the wayside much poorer.

Nell, too, was held up by one Pat O'Bryan, who, after taking her money, asked for something else for himself (he probably had to divide his spoils). Nell burst into laughter and gave him a kiss. O'Bryan was so taken aback that he returned her rings and was about to leave when Nell gave him ten guineas.

Nell was one of the people. She was magnanimous and generous of spirit because she had what she wanted. She knew she had risen far and she left no one behind. What she had she shared, even handing out sixpence to beggars who knocked at her door. And why not? She was enjoying her life with the King and their sons. The boys were growing up – Charles was four and James three and she would often take them to watch their father play tennis, or take them around the city to see the sights.

In January 1575 she bought a fine sedan chair with gold carving, for £34 11s, for her own trips out. Buckingham's father, the 1st duke, had made them popular, but it had caused a scandal to begin with as having a chair carried by two men was likened to using Englishmen as slaves. Nell delighted in being in the public eye – she had been an actress after all – but she also had friends to visit. Even though she now had her own sedan, she sometimes used chairs for hire. Anything was better than taking a boat along the Thames. Although this was a popular form of transport at the time it could be perilous for ladies in their fine dresses which inevitably got wet and covered in mud. One account lists her visits to Mrs Knight, Madam Young, the King's seamstress, Madam Churchill, Lady Sandys and Rose and the length of time the sedan carriers had to wait for her, sometimes as long as eleven hours. There must have been a lot to gossip about!

In February 1675 there was a court masque organised by the Queen. She wanted to cheer up her nieces, Mary and Anne, the Duke of York's daughters by his first wife, by giving them parts in *Calisto*, a play by John Crowne. Many of Nell's friends and acquaintances took part, including her former rival Moll Davis who had left the stage in 1668 but must have still been close to the King. It was performed over thirty times and Nell saw it on occasion. She may not have been on the stage any more but she still loved the theatre and took any opportunity to perform privately for the King or provide entertainment for his guests.

In the summer Philip William, Prince of Neuberg, arrived in England on a state visit. Nell dressed up one evening as an Arcadian shepherdess and danced for their pleasure. Both the Queen and Louise were there but Nell was delighting everyone by being the belle of the ball. She danced herself into a sweat, and, telling her audience it was much too hot, she flung open the windows to let in a delicious night breeze. Catherine and Louise sat and shivered. Unperturbed and caught up in the moment, Nell led Charles and the prince, as well as the other guests, into St James's Park to continue the revelries.

Not content to stop there, the next day Nell thought it would be a great idea to go to Hampton Court and so they boarded several barges and sailed up the Thames. While everyone else was content to laze around after the excesses of the previous night, Nell took the prince and the King fishing. Baronne d'Aulnoy, one of the prince's entourage, tells us of a treat Nell had in store:

> One of her schemes, which was previously arranged, proved very amusing. She suggested to the King that they might stop awhile, the better to enjoy the beauty of the evening and music; this done she had some fishing tackle produced; it was all painted and gilded, the Nets were silk, the Hooks gold. Every one commenced to fish, & the king was one of the most eager. He had already thrown in his line many times & was surprised at not catching anything. The Ladies rallied him, but calling out that they must not tease, he triumphantly showed his line to the end of which half a dozen fried Sprats were attached by a piece of silk! They burst into laughter in which all the Court joined, but Nelly said it was only right that a great king should have unusual Privileges! A Poor Fisherman could only take Fish alive but his Majesty caught them ready to eat![23]

Prince Philip also had a catch but his was very special indeed. When he reeled in his line he found a golden purse attached by silk threads containing a gold locket complete with a miniature of one of the court beauties. He returned the gift by sending her some expensive lace when he returned home.

Nell was exciting, impulsive, a born entertainer and her parties at Pall Mall – a meeting place for all of the Merry Gang – were well known to make a dull evening brighter. Soirées and supper parties were a regular occurrence at her new home and here Nell outdid herself. Food and drink was ordered in large amounts. She had a well-stocked cellar full of whisky, beer and wine – lots of wine. In Hopkin's biography, he calculates that in six months 1,008 gallons of ale and beer were consumed, working out at around 42 pints a day. That was some serious entertaining! The King was especially partial to a few glasses of canary – a sweet, fortified tipple. For an evening meal there would be a large buffet of nine or ten courses that might include duckling, beef, geese, oysters, rabbit, chicken, salmon, hare, partridge and the King's favourite, pigeon pie. Like the Queen, who is credited with bringing the drink to England, she also enjoyed tea and gave afternoon parties with copious refreshments.

As well as a rich menu of food, there would be evening entertainments of music, dancing, and song. On one occasion the actor and singer Henry Bowman was invited to perform for Nell, the King and the Duke of York. After his show, Nell reminded the King to give him something for his trouble. Charles, as usual, had no money and asked his brother for some coin. James too had no money and it was down to Nell to compensate Henry for his time.[24]

Nell's mother and sister – whose husband, John Cassells, died in 1675 – were living with her at this time. Nell was always generous with her money and paid for her brother-in-law's funeral and some new clothes for Rose. Did Nell hide away her drunken mother when she was entertaining for the evening? She doesn't seem the type of girl to be embarrassed by her family, but her mother had shamed her with her behaviour before. Rose had known the King's friends as well as Nell so perhaps she was still invited. She would go on to marry Guy Foster (or Forster), of whom little is known. There were certainly meetings and suppers to which they would not be invited as the King often used Nell's house as neutral ground for meetings of a political nature.

Nell's mother was unwell, as her apothecary bills show. Nell footed the bills for plasters, plague water and glysters for her mother and cordial julep with pearls for her eldest son. The youngest would take pectoral syrup for his chest and then there were purging powders, syrup of violets, balsamic pills, rhubarb, oil of nutmeg, gillyflower syrup, liquorice juice and plasters for toothache. Nell, though in good health, treated herself to rosewater, oil of lilies and white roses and Queen of Hungary's water to maintain her complexion.

*****

Nell asked little of the King but she did hope for more. Louise had been angling for some time for her son to be ennobled. Barbara, who had been keeping to herself for the most part and entertaining other lovers, also wanted titles for her own sons. But whose son would take precedence? Both of the King's mistresses wanted their son created first and Charles had to endure many an argument trying to placate them. To keep the peace, he assured them that their son's ennoblement would happen at the same time.

Danby was responsible for signing the patents so it really came down to which one he signed and authorised first. Louise was desperate it would be her son, so, after hearing the treasurer was about to travel to Bath, she sent her lawyer over to him on the night of his departure and gained his signature. Barbara arrived the next day to a locked house. Louise had won this round and on 9 August 1675, when Louise's son was three, he was made Duke of Richmond, Earl of March and Baron Settrington. His dukedom had become vacant after Charles' mistress Frances Stuart lost her husband, the previous duke of Richmond, in Denmark in 1672. Just a month later the infant was also created Duke of Lennox, Earl of Darnley, and Baron Methuen of Torbolten. Barbara had to wait until September and Danby's return before her son was made Duke of Grafton. The ennobling of these two boys put them in equal rank to the Duke of Monmouth, the King's eldest illegitimate son. There would be nothing yet for Nell's children and she was furious that Louise had got one up on her. She shouted at Charles, 'Even Barbara's brats were not made Dukes until they were twelve or thirteen, but this French spy's son is ennobled when little more than an infant in arms!'[25] She would not give up wanting more for her children and Charles would not hear the end of it for some time.

Nell had been given the position of Lady of the Queen's Privy Chamber, but it was a token role to enable her to draw a salary. She had no wish to embarrass the Queen by attending on her but it was an excuse to buy herself some new dresses. Danby was about to tighten the reigns on the King's expenditure. He was well aware that Charles' largest expense was keeping his mistresses. Nell came off worse out of all of them. Not for the pretty, witty actress the astonishing sum of £136,668 that Barbara received one year. Whilst Barbara's regular allowance was £6,000, Louise's was £8,600. Nell's previous allowance of £4,000 was increased to £5,000 – the extra £1,000 for her children – and with occasional secret service payments, she managed on around £10,000 a year. The secret service fund was dipped into for payments that no one would ever question.

Nell didn't actually work as a spy though her friend Aphra Behn, who would turn to playwriting and dedicate one to Nell, did. Louise on the other hand was reporting to France. Colbert de Croissy, the French ambassador, visited her daily, fishing for information. Whether she knew what she was doing or whether she purposefully passed on state secrets is a matter for debate. Charles would certainly have talked to her, but he knew of her allegiance to her own country and would not have been so foolish as to tell her anything significant. Being at Whitehall she would have picked up all sorts of information and perhaps it was these rumours that she passed on to Croissy, who in turn gave her gifts to show his appreciation. Later, when Barillon took over Croissy's position he told Louis XIV, 'The truth about her is, that she has shown great, constant and intelligent zeal for your Majesty's interests, and given me numberless useful hints and pieces of information.'[26]

Charles felt that sedition brewed in the now popular coffee houses. They were not only meeting places for drinking the newly imported beverage but also where debate, discussion, 'speaking evil' and the distribution of pamphlets took place. Political debate caused unrest and he felt the coffee houses were filled with 'idle and disaffected persons'[27] who could foment rebellion. The court, the King and his mistresses were all targets. Nell had noticed that on her sedan jaunts, coffee house patrons would jeer at her – it was not what she was used to being usually so popular. At the end of the year the King would issue a proclamation to try to shut them down and ban the sale of chocolate, teas and sherbert as well. It was extremely unpopular and ultimately didn't work. Even Nell's vicar from St Martin-in-the Fields asked her to talk to the King about it.

Nell knew that the main bone of contention with people was the cost of the King's mistresses. An early biographer tells of how the King complained to Nell of Parliament, his ministers, and Danby's control of funds and asked her, 'What shall I do to please the People of England?' Her response was to tell him, 'There is but one way left, which expedient I am afraid it will be difficult to persuade you to embrace ... Dismiss your ladies and mind your business; the People of England will soon be pleased.'[28] But Charles would never, could never give up his mistresses.

When Charles moaned that politics and people would not leave him alone, Nell suggested he give them a Scotch collop, French ragout and a calf's head, referring to Lauderdale, his Secretary of State for Scotland, Louise and Danby – who it was now rumoured were lovers. She rarely meddled with politics but a chance to get rid of the King's French mistress would have delighted her and she was about to irritate her even more.

Louise had spent the year chasing remedies for her affliction but when she heard Nell had finished the renovations on her bedroom – and what a glorious room it was – she burst into tears, and then, in a complete turnaround, decided to give a banquet. It doesn't appear that Nell was invited and Louise, in another bid to outdo her rival, stripped naked with two of her friends to entertain the King in her private closet. Charles couldn't resist and had an exceedingly pleasurable night while Nell fumed at home.

All of the mistresses' woes and worries, tiffs and troubles would soon pale when a new woman entered the King's orbit. In December 1675 Hortense Mancini, the daughter of Baron Lorenzo Mancini, an Italian aristocrat, and Girolama Mazarin, Cardinal Mazarin's sister, arrived in England. One of five sisters noted for their great beauty, Charles had met Hortense many years ago and even proposed to her, but her uncle, the late Cardinal Mazarin, France's previous chief minister, would not give them permission to marry. Instead, Hortense had unfortunately married the Duc de la Meilleraye, a religious fanatic who made her life hell with his bizarre jealousy and strange ways. In a frenetic rage, he destroyed his priceless art collection, painting over any nudity, especially bare breasts, and damaged sculptures by chipping off their nude parts. It was said that he had even had his female servants' teeth knocked out to make them unattractive to the opposite sex.

Hortense also bore the brunt of his obsessions and he frequently punished her for her sins as he imagined them. She would be locked away for hours to pray for forgiveness. He swore she had lovers tucked away in her rooms and would search them relentlessly. Little wonder then that after a time Hortense did take a lover. Her name was Sidonie de Courcelles. When the duke found out, his wife and her paramour were sequestered in a convent, but Hortense had had enough. In her memoirs she recalled: 'I could not speak to a servant but he was dismissed the same day. I could not receive two visits but he was forbidden in the house. if I showed any preference for one of my maids, she was at once taken from me. He would have liked me to see no one in the world except himself. Above all, he could not endure that I should see either his relations or my own – the latter because they had begun to take my part; his own, because they no more approved of his conduct than did mine.'[29]

She petitioned Louis XIV for a divorce, but in 1668, without her divorce being agreed, she escaped from the brutality of her marriage and travelled around Europe, disguised as a man. After a while she became the mistress of Duke Charles Emmanuel II of Savoy until his death in 1675. The duke was a married man and his wife would no longer tolerate his mistress sticking around. The English ambassador to France, Ralph

Montagu, suggested Hortense visit England to see her cousin, Mary of Modena, the Duke of York's new wife. Mary had unhappily married 'Dismal Jimmie' on 23 November 1673. She would be the King's brother's second wife after his first wife, Anne Hyde, died in 1671. It is said that when Mary first saw James, she burst into tears. He was twenty-five years older than her and no pretty picture to look at. However, mortified as she was, she had to marry him and the Duke of York was more than happy with his new Catholic bride. The people, however, were not so happy and when Mary arrived in England on Guy Fawkes day Evelyn noted, 'the youths of the city burnt the Pope in effigy, after they had made procession with it in great triumph, they being displeased at the Duke for altering his religion and marrying an Italian lady.'[30]

Hortense thought Montagu's suggestion was a good idea, so, dressed as a Cavalier, and with her black pageboy rescued from a Mediterranean corsair, and a few other servants in tow, she set sail for England. Charles, the ever-affable King, welcomed her to court, gave her apartments close to her pregnant cousin and arranged for her to have an allowance of £4,000 a year. Nell would soon have another rival.

Engraving of Nell as Cupid by Richard Tompson, after a painting by Peter Cross. (Wikimedia Commons, public domain)

'Nell' Eleanor Gwyn (Gwynne) (1651–1687), Anonymous, c.1670-1699. (Wikimedia Commons, public domain)

Study for a Portrait of a Woman by Sir Peter Lely, c.1670s. (Metropolitan Museum of Art, CC1.0)

Right: Charles II. (Wellcome Collection, CC4.0)

Below: Bagnigge Wells: the exterior, with heaps of wood and stone in the foreground. Etching by C. J. Smith, 1844. (Wellcome Collection, CC4.0)

Catherine of Braganza, consort of King Charles II. Mezzotint by H. H. Quiter after P. Lely, 1678. (Wikimedia Commons, public domain)

Engraving of Samuel Pepys by Robert White, after a portrait by Sir Godfrey Kneller. (Wikimedia Commons, public domain)

Charles II, Nell and Evelyn (Scene – St. James's Park). From a painting by E. M. Ward, A.R.A., 1852. (Wikimedia Commons, public domain)

Above: Covent
Garden in the reign of
Charles the Second.
Compiled from
pictures, drawings,
prints and descriptions
(Wikimedia Commons,
public domain).

Left: Charles Beauclerk
(1670–1726),
Duke of St. Albans
by Sir Godfrey
Kneller, c. 1690–95
(Metropolitan Museum
of Art, CC1.0).

Nell at her lodgings-door in Drury Lane. The Maypole in the Strand restored, illustration in Cunningham's biography, 1852. (Wikimedia Commons, public domain)

Eleanor Gwynne print by Abraham de Blois after Sir Peter Lely. (Rijksmuseum, CC1.0)

Above: Nell Gwynne by Charles Landseer, 1879. (Smithsonian Institute, CC0)

Right: Eleanor ('Nell') Gwynne (1650-1687), mistress of King Charles II of England. The caption to this image noted that 'Bobbed hair was not as fashionable in the days of Charles II'. (Smithsonian Institute, CC0)

Laurence Hyde, First Earl of Rochester. Engraving by Jacobus Houbraken after Sir Godfrey Kneller, 1741. (Yale Center for British Art, Paul Mellon Collection, public domain)

John Wilmot, 2nd
Earl of Rochester,
Anonymous, c. 1600
and 1699. (Wikimedia
Commons, public
domain)

Barbara Villiers, Countess of
Castlemaine and Duchess of
Cleveland (1640-1709), Anonymous,
c. 1665 and 1680. (Wikimedia
Commons, public domain)

Portrait of Hortense Mancini, Duchesse de Mazarin (1646-1699), half-length, in the guise of Aphrodite, Follower of Jacob Ferdinand Voet, c.1700 (Wikimedia Commons, public domain)

Louise de Kéroualle, Duchess of Portsmouth (1649–1734) by Henri Gascar, c. between 1670 and 1701. (Wikimedia Commons, public domain)

Louise de Kéroualle, Duchess of Portsmouth (1649-1734), Anonymous, c. between 1700 and 1799. (Wikimedia Commons, public domain)

Cartoon showing Charles II and the Fire, undated, unknown artist, seventeenth century. (Yale Center for British Art, Paul Mellon Collection, public domain)

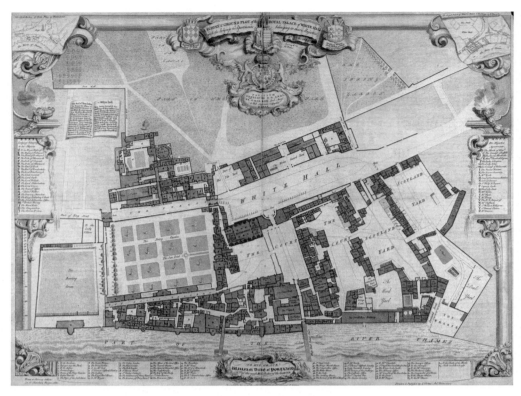

A Survey & Ground Plot of the Royal Palace at Whitehall, George Vertue. (Yale Center for British Art, Paul Mellon Collection, public domain)

Windsor Castle from the South, Oil on canvas, unknown artist, perhaps Jan Griffier the Elder, after Jan Vorsterman, after 1681, seventeenth century. (Yale Center for British Art, Paul Mellon Collection, public domain)

THE GREAT PLAGUE: THE MANIAC PRONOUNCING THE DOOM OF LONDON. *(See p. 216.)*

A man in rags announcing the forthcoming doom, during the great plague in London. Wood engraving by A.B. Frost. (Wellcome Collection, CC4.0)

Above: The Death of
Buckingham by Augustus
Leopold Egg, undated,
exhibited 1855. (Yale Center
for British Art, Paul Mellon
Collection, public domain)

Left: King James II; table with
a crown in the background.
Engraving by P. Landry, 1693.
(Wellcome Collection, CC4.0)

Chapter Six

Plots, Intrigues and Scandals
1676-1678

Barbara, Duchess of Cleveland, the King's oldest mistress, was no longer in favour. Her relationship with the King was nothing like it had been in the early days of the Restoration and they spent little time together. He would always care for her and their children, as he cared for all his women and their offspring, but now Barbara decided it was time for a new life. The court no longer welcomed her as it once did. It was time to move to France. Nell hosted a leaving party for her in March 1676. Their relationship had had its ups and downs but Nell held no lasting animosity towards her. After all, she was with the King now.

With Barbara living in Paris, Charles now spent most of his time with Nell, although she did have to share him with his new mistress, Hortense. Louise was left out and feeling terrible. She had put on a lot of weight and felt unattractive, earning the nickname of Fubbs or Fubbsy (Chubby) from the King. She spent her days moping and weeping and banged her head against her bedpost, giving herself a black eye. Deciding to leave court for a time, she travelled down to Bath where the King occasionally visited her.

In August the French ambassador reported, 'Yesterday evening I saw something which aroused all my pity ... I went to see Madame de Portsmouth. She opened her heart to me in the presence of two of her maids ... Madame de Portsmouth explained to me what grief the frequent visits of the King of England to Madame de Sussex cause her every day ... two girls remained propped against the wall with downcast eyes; their mistress let loose a torrent of tears. Sobs and sighs interrupted her speech. Indeed, I have never beheld a sadder or more touching sight.'[1]

Nell might have felt some sympathy for the 'weeping willow' – another one of her nicknames for Louise. The King came to her for supper but left in the evening for Hortense's house. Hortense originally stayed at one of the Duke of York's properties in St James's Park until Charles gave her a house of her own in Chelsea. She was definitely flavour of the month, but Nell shrugged off her own feelings and turned it into another opportunity to send up Louise. Wearing black mourning clothes, she told everyone she was going into mourning for the death of all of Louise's hopes and dreams. Hortense, added to the mix of mistresses, created a rivalry between the three women that became the talk of the court and something else for the rumour mill to latch on to.

Edmund Waller wrote a poem, *The Triple Combat*, which captured their rivalry, and Nell put in an appearance as Chloris.

> Venus had been an equal friend to both,
> And victory to declare herself seems loth;
> Over the camp, with doubtful wings, she flies,
> Till Chloris shining in the field she spies.
> The lovely Chloris well-attended came,
> A thousand Graces waited on the dame;
> Her matchless form made all the English glad,
> And foreign beauties less assurance had;
> Yet, like the Three on Ida's top, they all
> Pretend alike, contesting for the ball...[2]

A more ribald verse put it more plainly:

> Since Cleveland is fled till she's brought to bed,
> And Nelly is quite forgotten,
> And Mazarine is as old as the Queen,
> And Portsmouth, the young whore, is rotten.[3]

But Hortense was a wild card and would not remain faithful to the King, shockingly having an affair with his daughter by Barbara Villiers. Anne became the Countess of Sussex at the tender age of thirteen when she married Thomas Lennard, the Count of Sussex, in August 1674 at Hampton Court Palace. It was an uneasy match. Sussex wanted his wife to live a life of rural isolation at his ancestral home but Anne hated the countryside. Instead she stayed at Whitehall in her mother's apartments and gave birth to her daughter, Barbara, there in July. Hortense began visiting Anne, who was soon enthralled. Here was a woman who had travelled Europe, dressed in men's clothes, and was entertaining and fun to be with. Anne fell desperately in love.

When her mother heard the scandalous news of her daughter's affair, she sent letter after letter to Charles telling him to do something about it. When it came to men, same-sex relationships were illegal and punishable by death, but lesbianism (or tribadism) was not, although it could be frowned upon by family and friends. It was Anne's husband who stormed into Whitehall looking for his wife, intent on stopping their relationship. Despite Anne's protests, he took her back to their home and estate at Herstmonceux in Sussex. Devastated at being taken from the court and her lover, Anne took to her bed, refusing to get up, and spent long days with a picture of Hortense beside her, weeping and kissing the image of her lover.

It wasn't the only same-sex relationship that Hortense had. Nell's friend Aphra Behn, the playwright, was also enamoured of Hortense, and her introduction to *The History of the Nun* suggests they had a close relationship:

> to the Most Illustrious Princess, The Dutchess of Mazarine ... how infinitely one of Your own Sex ador'd You, and that, among all the numerous Conquest, Your Grace has made over the Hearts of Men, Your Grace had not subdu'd a more intire Slave; I assure you, Madam, there is neither Compliment, nor Poetry, in this humble Declaration, but a Truth, which has cost me a great deal of Inquietude, for that Fortune has not set me in such a Station, as might justifie my Pretence to the honour and satisfaction of being ever near Your Grace, to view eternally that lovely Person, and here that surprising Wit; what can be more grateful to a Heart, than so great, and so agreeable, an Entertainment? And how few Objects are there, that can render it so entire a Pleasure, as at once to hear you speak, and to look upon your Beauty?[4]

Behn also wrote of same-sex love in her poem *To The Fair Clorinda*: 'When so much beauteous Woman is in view/ Against thy Charms we struggle but in vain.'[5] Her relationship with Nell may also have been based on more than platonic feelings on her part but Nell only had eyes for the King.

In the autumn Charles and Nell went to Newmarket. When he was Prince of Wales, he had often visited the town with his father and it held special memories for him. The Civil War curtailed racing at Newmarket so when Charles was restored to power he had a new palace, stables and course built. Charles loved horse racing and famously took part himself, winning on 14 October 1671 – the only monarch to ever ride a winner. Today, the Rowley Mile Course commemorates the King's nickname and the name of his favourite racehorse, Old Rowley, and his mistress is remembered by the Nell Gwyn Stakes. Tales tell of a secret passage that ran from the palace to Nell's house, as in every town where the King and Nell had properties. Over the years they would spend many days at Newmarket together, sometimes accompanied by their son, Charles, who became an accomplished rider.

On their return to London, the King heard some troubling news. If Hortense hadn't caused enough trouble with the Countess of Sussex, she had now by having an affair with Louis I de Grimaldi, the Prince of Monaco, earning her the title 'the Italian whore'. Charles loved his women and he had had many of them over the years, but he did expect a degree of fidelity from the ones that were closest to his heart. He was furious to find out that his latest mistress had taken a lover, so furious that he stopped her allowance (though, always a soft touch where women were concerned, he soon renewed her payment). However, his relationship with Hortense would never be quite the same again. They would remain friends but the King's attention turned back to Nell and Louise, who was delighted to be back in favour.

Nell probably found it all amusing but she was about to show her serious side. All the other mistresses' children had been ennobled and now she wanted a title for her eldest child. Nell is supposed to have called out to little Charles, 'Come hither, you little bastard!' to the shock of the King. When Charles rebuked her for saying such a thing, she craftily told him that she had no other name to call him by. Another less likely story has her holding little Charles by the legs and dangling him out of the top floor window at 79 Pall Mall. When the King heard the child's screams, he remonstrated with Nell, who threatened to drop him if he didn't receive a title. In response the King shouted, 'God save the Earl of Burford!'

Whatever truly happened, their son was made Baron Heddington and Earl of Burford on 27 December 1676, with a £1,000 a year allowance.

Nell was delighted and threw a lavish party for young Charles. The King also promised to give his son the office of Registrar in Chancery. There would be no title for little James, but the boys would finally be given the surname of Beauclerk. Nell was given the duty on log exports and the promise of the freehold on 79 Pall Mall, making it the only house on the south side of Pall Mall that didn't belong to the Crown. And soon she would also have her own coat of arms.

In January 1677 the three rivals met under a pretext of friendship. This was the time for exchanging gifts and Nell brought boxes of chocolates – reassuring Louise and Hortense they weren't like the ones she had given Moll Davis! The three women swopped pleasantries, complimenting each other and congratulating Nell on her son's ennoblement, although probably through gritted teeth as the French ambassador put it, 'Everything passed off with great merriment and with many civilities from one to the other, but I do not suppose in all England it would be possible to get together three people more obnoxious to each other.'[6]

Nell made the most of the situation:

> [She] who was of the bold, laughing sort, turned round to
> De Courtin and asked why it was that the King of France did
> not send presents to her, instead of to the Weeping Willow
> who had just gone out? She vowed that he would have no
> profit in doing so, because the King of England was her
> constant nocturnal companion, and liked her far the best.
> The other ladies had heard of the luxurious fineness of
> Miss Nelly's under-clothing, and asked if they could judge
> of it for themselves. Without more ado she let them raise
> each petticoat, one by one, and before all the room examine
> them on her.[7]

The talk of underclothes astounded Courtin – did all women not wear the same thing? Nell emphatically denied it and made sure he had a good look at hers. He wrote to Pomponne, the French Foreign Minister, 'Never in my life did I see such cleanliness, neatness and sumptuousness. I should speak of other things which were also shown if M. de Lionne were still Foreign Secretary, but with you I must be more grave and decorous.'[8] Pomponne replied, 'I am sure you forgot all your troubles when you were making Mistris Nesle raise those neat and magnificent petticoats of hers.'[9] Nell's undergarments were crisp and white, Louise, however, often had dirty petticoats and Hortense rarely wore them, preferring trousers. She may have flirted with him but the French ambassador hoped that Nell could be persuaded to help their cause by promoting a return to Catholicism. Nell must have told him in no uncertain terms she was no Louise as he had to report back that they would get no joy there.

In February one of Nell's true friends would be in trouble. The Duke of Buckingham was a political agitator, part of a group known as the 'Country Party' that opposed the Court Party. When Parliament convened on the fifteenth, Buckingham gave a speech, saying that since Parliament had not met in fifteen months, it was in effect dissolved. He called for a new Parliament, ending with, 'My Motion therefore to your Lordships shall be, that we humbly address ourselves to his Majesty, and beg of him, for his own sake, as well as for all the people's sakes, to give as speedily a new Parliament.'[10]

It was a step too far for the King. Buckingham and the men who supported him – Shaftesbury, Salisbury and Wilson – were called to account and told to apologise. When the three lords refused, they were sent to the Tower of London. Buckingham, however, had made a getaway along the Thames by boat. Guards were sent to find him, searching his house and questioning his servants, but no one knew his whereabouts. When Parliament met the next day, it was agreed if he was not found by noon, the ports would be closed and the search stepped up. To everyone's amazement, Buckingham, as calm as anything, walked into the room and took his seat. He too refused to apologise for 'thinking and speaking his thoughts',[11] but did offer an apology to the King and Parliament. It was not good enough and he was committed to the Tower.

Nell looked for advice from her old flame Charles Buckhurst, who had been made Earl of Dorset, and he suggested she visit Buckingham, giving her a note for him which read, 'The best woman in the world brings you this paper, and, at this time, the discreetest. Pray, my lord, resign your understanding and your interest wholly to her conduct.'[12]

Nell duly made her way to the Tower and advised Buckingham to put it all down on paper. If he had upset her by trying to bed her before, it was all now forgiven. Nell would support him through thick and thin. Buckingham wrote a heartfelt letter to the king:

I am so surprised with what Mrs Nelly has told me, that I know not in the world what to say. The more sensible grief I had in being put away from Your Majesty, was not the losing my place, but the being shout out of Your Majesty's kindness. And if the aspiring to that be a fault, it is at least a more pardonable one than the aspiring to wealth and making one's own fortune. What has made this inclination more violent in me, than perhaps it is in other people, is the honour I had of being bred up with Your Majesty from a child; for those affections are ever strongest in men, which begin in their youngest years. And therefore I beseech Your Majesty to believe me when I say, that I have ever loved you more than all the rest of mankind; and that I have not only once chosen to follow you in misfortune rather than be in ever so great plenty any other way but that I would willingly do so again tomorrow, if Your Majesty could take it kindly of me.

What should I say? I am not one that pretends to a preciseness in devotion, but yet I am sure Your Majesty never found me to be a knave and I wish that all the curses imaginable may fall upon me, if I tell you a lie; or if I would tell you a lie to save my life. I have lived long enough in the world, not to care much for it, and have met with so much ungratefulness from almost all mankind, that the pleasure of conversing with man is one quite taken from me. Yet I beseech Your Majesty to believe, that the grief which in my whole life did ever sit nearest to my heart, was the loss of Your Majesty's kindness. You that have been a lover yourself, know what it is to think oneself ill-used by a mistress that one loves extremely and it is that only I can truly compare my great misfortune to. Yet there was besides my own misfortune in it, a great deal of art used to make me believe Your Majesty hated me, and I can hardly forgive them that did it, since it was done with as much undutifulness to Your majesty, as ingratitude to me.

But why should I say any more of this matter? What you have been pleased to say to Mrs Nelly, is ten thousand times more than ever I can deserve. Could you make a question whether I can love you or no? Oh Christ sir for heavens sake know that I would as willingly die tomorrow to do your Majesty's service, as any of those about you would have me dead, to satisfy their envy and their ill nature. I am really in that ecstasy of joy, and so truly satisfied with my condition, since I am persuaded your Majesty has a kindness for me, that I would willingly stay here all my life if your Majesty can think it may be for your service. Though I confess I should be very glad to throw myself at your majesty's feet, and give you humble thanks for the goodness you have been pleased to show me. In short sir, do with me what you please, I will absolutely be governed by you.[13]

His plea worked and he was back dining with Charles by August, and visiting Nell, who, though she was delighted to see him out of the Tower, was fed up with his uncleanliness and advised him to buy 'new shoes, that he might not dirty her rooms, and a new periwig that she might not smell him stink two storeys high when he knocks at the outward door.'[14]

There were several attempts to get Nell back on the stage. The actors and audience missed her and her replacements never made up for the pretty, witty actress' absence. Aphra Behn wanted her to play the part of Angelica in her play, *The Rover*; Samuel Pordage offered her the part of Thalestris in *The Stage of Babylon*, Wycherley wanted her to do *The Country Wife* and her old friend John Dryden wanted her desperately for his new play *All For Love*, even saying she could have a year to practise. But she turned them all down.

Nell thought, perhaps, that if she did not return to the stage it would make her more acceptable as a lady. She was still angling for a title herself. Barbara and Louise had been ennobled by the King, and Frances and Hortense had their own titles, so why couldn't she? The King thought it reasonable enough – perhaps a lesser title of countess would suit – Countess of Greenwich even. He ran it past Danby, Lord High Treasurer, who in no uncertain terms shut down the idea. Nell was absolutely furious and 'at perfect defiance with him.'[15] She had never liked Danby and knew he favoured the other mistresses, especially Louise, more than her. Danby made her feel like she was not good enough. Even after she had come so far, this man trod her dreams back down in the dirt. When Charles visited her one evening, she could contain her anger no longer and spat out choice words about the King's Lord High Treasurer. Danby was informed and he wrote to his wife, 'Remember to send to see my Lord Burford without any message to Nelly, and when Mrs Turner is with you, bid her tell Nelly that you wonder why he should be your Lord's enemy that has always been kind to her, but you wonder more to find her supporting only those who are known to be the King's enemies, for in that you are sure she does very ill.'[16] Nell of course was not friends with the King's enemies. She would do nothing to jeopardise her position. Danby on the other hand had placed Mrs Turner in Nell's household to spy on her.

One of Nell's oldest friends, the Earl of Rochester, had taken an actress, Elizabeth Barry as his mistress although he had done far more by training, coaching and supporting her to become one of the greatest actresses of the Restoration age. Nell also helped by passing on her expertise. Barry's stage debut in 1674 had been a disaster, 'several persons of wit and quality being at the play and observing how she performed positively gave their opinion she would never be capable of any part of acting,'[17] but Rochester had moulded her into something special with his private lessons and had also taken her to his bed.

In December 1677 Barry gave birth to Rochester's daughter. It seems that the earl was not providing for his mistress and child and Nell bought the baby's layette. Henry Savile, one of Charles' Merry Gang and great friends with Rochester and Nell, had been the Duke of York's Groom of the Bedchamber from 1665 to 1672, and Charles' from 1673. He informed Rochester of the situation. 'The greatest news I can send you from hence is what the King told me last night, that your Lordship has a daughter borne by the body of Mrs Barry of which I give your honour joy. I doubt she does not lie in much state, for a friend and protectress of hers in the Mall (Nell) was much lamenting her poverty very lately, not without some gentle reflections on your Lordship's want either of generosity or bowels towards a lady who had not refused you the full enjoyment of her charms.'[18]

But Rochester was severely ill with syphilis, 'almost blind, utterly lame, and scarce within the hopes of ever seeing London again,'[19] and in financial difficulties. He wrote to Barry of his continued affection, but not long after found she was having an affair. He would take his daughter Elizabeth away from her, telling her she 'made it so absolutely necessary … to do so,'[20] but little is known of his daughter's life apart from that she died young. Barry, however, would act in hundreds of plays and have a career that spanned thirty-five years.

Rochester, still a young man, was suffering from living life to the full and more. Sex, drink and violent bouts of rowdiness were catching up with him. He had been in disgrace in 1675 for what was termed the 'sundial affair'. After a day of drinking with Buckhurst and others of the Merry Gang in the King's apartments, they took a turn about the Privy Gardens. Here was an astronomical device, designed by Father Francis Hall, which was Charles' treasured possession. Made as a '...fountain of glass spheres, or a giant candelabrum with tiered, branching arms ending in crystal globes,'[21] it suffered the brunt of a debauched day.

Rochester, who though the thing looked rather phallic, shouted out, 'Dost thou stand there to fuck time?' and proceeded to smash it into smithereens. Not only had he destroyed the King's property but it had also contained images of the King, Queen, Duke of York, Prince Rupert and the King's mother. Once he had sobered up, Rochester, realising what he had done, fled to the countryside. Charles of course was furious and so enraged he himself disappeared for a few days to cool down. When Rochester was forgiven he got drunk with Henry Savile and danced around a fountain naked.

But then there was an incident at Epsom. On another bender with his companions and one Captain Downs, they called for music, but when the musicians wouldn't play, they trussed them up in blankets and tossed them around. A constable tried to stop the chaos and was beaten for interfering. He escaped and called the watch who, satisfied that the situation had calmed down, left them to it, but Rochester drew his sword and attacked the constable again. Captain Downs tried to save the constable from certain death at the end of Rochester's sword, but when the watch returned they thought Downs was the culprit and hit him with a pole. When he tried to defend himself, he was fatally wounded with a pike. Here was another death at the hands of the King's friends and yet again there were no trials, no imprisonment and no executions.

Instead of returning to court when he was allowed to return to London, Rochester pretended he was Alexander Bendo, an Italian, or as de Gramont, the memoirist, put it in his account of Rochester's antics, he was a German who dressed in a black cloak decorated with zodiac signs, 'an antique cap, a great reverend beard and a magnificent false medal set round with glittering pearls, rubies and diamonds, hung about his neck in a massy goldlike chain,'[22] to deliver his predictions. Nell was complicit in promoting his latest prank.

> He retreated into one of the most obscure corners of the city; where, again changing both his name and his dress, in order to act a new part he caused bills to be dispersed, giving notice, of "The recent arrival of a famous German doctor, who, by long application and experience, had found out wonderful secrets, and infallible remedies." His secrets consisted in knowing what was past, and foretelling what was to come, by the assistance of astrology: and the virtue of his remedies principally consisted in giving present relief to unfortunate young women in all manner of diseases, and all kinds of accidents incident to the fair sex, either from too unbounded charity to their neighbours, or too great indulgence to themselves.[23]

For a month he plied his trade at lodgings in Tower Street next to the Black Swan and Nell gave out his advertising (see Appendix III). The historian Burnet thought there was something far more sinister going on and that Rochester was using it as a ruse for unbridled sex and impregnating women who went to him for a cure for infertility.

What Nell thought of Rochester's antics we can't be sure. He must have amused her at times, and exasperated her at others, but she would remain his faithful friend and he hers. When his lifestyle caught up with him, he retired to his country seat. Nell missed him, but there was a surprise entertainment in mid-December, when a group of French actors visited the court. They had been on their way to Spain when they were shipwrecked off the coast of Dover. Nell welcomed them to her home one evening and put on one of her lavish suppers. They also played at Whitehall and the King was rather taken with their fifteen-year-old star, 'who had more beauty and sweetness than ever was seen on the stage since a friend of ours (Nell) left it.'[24]

All the entertaining, not to mention her gambling debts, had put a strain on Nell's finances and she was feeling the pinch, contrary to Burnet stating she was 'maintained at vast expense.'[25] She knew Danby would not help her but her friend Sir Robert Howard was secretary to the Treasury and he tried to negotiate on her behalf. As Nell had thought, Danby would not be helping her out anytime soon.

Irish pensions were paid to some of the court wits, including Rochester and Buckingham. It was a contentious issue and Arthur Capel, Lord Lieutenant of Ireland between 1672 and 1677, went some way to block payments and grants to the King's mistresses. Barbara had asked for Phoenix Park but was refused. Some payments to Louise were also blocked. Nell had been granted an £800 pension, but it was not forthcoming. Rochester wrote to Capel as her trustee, hoping his influence would have a favourable outcome: 'The bearer of this being to present your Excellence with a preference from your King, wherein my name is to appear, it becomes my duty to let you know that I am made use of only as a trustee for Mrs Nelly & that by a particular direction your favour is humbly begg'd and much rely'd upon by her in this affayre.'[26]

Rochester's name didn't count for anything in this case. Howard knew that Nell and her sister were entitled to revenue from some Irish estates, but these were currently being blocked by the Irish Court of Claims. He was advised to have her included in the Irish Civil List and wrote to the new Lord Lieutenant of Ireland, the Duke of Ormond, 'Mrs Nelly has commanded me to present her amongst your true servants and does think herself so much obliged to Your Excellency, that unless within a little time you command her something that she may serve you in, she swears she will pick a quarrel with you, for she vows she loves you entirely.'[27]

Nell was content that at least there would be some financial help, but in December her old pal Harry Killigrew upset her with a night-time visit to her house. Harry was another notorious young man who had a penchant for getting into trouble. The son of Thomas Killigrew, the theatre manager, Harry had gained a place as Groom of the Bedchamber to the Duke of York but had been sent to France after he attacked the Duke of Buckingham. Killigrew had been in love, or lust, with Anna Maria Brudenell, Countess of Shrewsbury, whom some suggested as having an 'evil pre-eminence.'[28] She took her lovers and tossed them aside. Killigrew was one of them and he was not happy, letting loose 'all his abusive eloquence against her ladyship: he attacked her with the most bitter invectives from head to foot: he drew a frightful picture of her conduct; and turned all her personal charms, which he used to extol, into defects.'[29] The countess was Buckingham's mistress at the time and when Buckingham saw him at the theatre, he 'did soundly beat and take away his sword, and make a fool of, till the fellow prayed him to spare his life.'[30]

Charles had Killigrew sent to the Tower, but because he was so sore and injured, he was allowed home to recuperate with the undertaking he would attend an enquiry. Instead he fled to France. It was said the Countess of Shrewsbury followed him there, intent on finishing him off. He was still causing trouble when he returned from exile in 1669 and told all who would listen that he had slept with Buckingham's whore. He was attacked as he left his home at Turnham Green and left for dead with nine wounds. His servant was killed. Buckingham admitted to the King he had his hand in it, but his hired thugs 'did not mean to hurt but to beat him and he did run first at them with his sword.'[31]

Killigrew's wife, Anne Savage, had died in October 1677 and Nell knew it would not be long before he went off the rails. Louise had been severely ill and many feared or gleefully anticipated, her death, but she recovered. Harry thought he should deliver the news to Nell at four in the morning, completely inebriated. He woke her up by banging on the door and shouting for her to come down. He said he had a message from the King. When Nell told him in no uncertain terms to curb his behaviour, he preceded to loudly abuse her. When Charles heard what he had done, he was banished from court – again. He may have helped out Nell's sister many years ago but he was nothing but trouble now. To add to her woes, Nell was burgled in January 1678. They stole her wonderful engraved silver plate and despite offering a reward in *The London Gazette,* it was never recovered.

Barbara was back briefly in the spring of 1678. She was having an affair with the Marquis de Chatillon, one of Louis XIV's gentlemen of the bedchamber, and their love letters had found their way to the King. The culprit was Ralph Montagu, the English ambassador to France, who had also been her lover. Charles was unfazed at her exploits, but when she returned to France she also found that Montagu had been having an affair with her daughter, Anne (who had also been in love with Hortense Mancini and was now living in France). She immediately wrote to Charles:

> I was never so surprised in my whole life-time as I was
> at my coming hither, to find my Lady Sussex gone from

my house and monastery where I left her, and this letter from her, which I here send you the copy of. I never in my whole life-time heard of such government of herself as she has had since I went into England. She has never been in the monastery two days together, but every day gone out with the Ambassador (Ralph Montagu), and has often lain four days together at my house, and sent for her meat to the Ambassador; he being always with her till five o'clock in the morning, they two shut up together alone, and would not let my maitre d'hôtel wait, nor any of my servants, only the Ambassador's. This has made so great a noise at Paris, that she is now the whole discourse. I am so much afflicted that I can hardly write this for crying, to see a child that I doted on as I did on her, should make me so ill a return, and join with the worst of men to ruin me.[32]

She wanted something done about Montagu, and the ambassador, feeling he should explain himself to the King, travelled back to London where Charles promptly had him dismissed from his post.

Charles must have talked through this latest debacle with Nell, who was ever ready to be his sounding board. In June, with the King's consent, she was preparing to send her youngest son, James, to school in Paris even though he was only six (her oldest son, Charles, may have been schooled at Eton and spent some time being tutored in France). Nothing is known of where James went to school in the French capital or who he lived with at the time. His mother mentioned him in her letter to Laurence (Lory) Hyde, the second son of Edward Hyde, 1st Earl of Clarendon, and brother to the Duke of York's first wife, which was also filled with the latest gossip. It was written by her secretary but brings Nell alive on the page:

Pray Deare Mr Hide forgive me for not writeing to you before now for the reasone is I have bin sick thre months & sinse I recoverd I have had nothing to intertaine you withal not have nothing now worth writing but that I can holde no longer to let you know I have never ben in any companie without drinking your health for I love you with all my soule. The pel mel is now to me a dismal plase sinse I have so utterly lost Sr Car Scrope never to be recooverd agane for he tould me he could not live allwayes at this rate & so begune to be a little uncivil, which I could not suffer from an ugly baux garson. Ms Knights Lady mothers dead & she has put up a scuthin no beiger then my lady grins scunchis. Mylord Rochester is gon in the cuntrei. Mr Savil has got a misfortune, but is upon recovery & is to marry an hairess who I thinke wont have an ill time ont if he holds up his thumb. My lord of Dorscit apiers wonse in thre munths, for he drinkes aile with Shadwell & Mr Haris at the Dukes house all day long. my Lord Burford remembers his sarvis to you. my lord Bauclaire is is goeing into france. we are going to supe with the king at whithall & my lady Harvie. the King remebers his sarvis to you. now lets talke of state affairs, for we never caried things so cunningly as now for we don't know whether we shall have pesce or war, but I am for war and for no toher reason but that you may come home. I have a thousand merry conseets, but I cant make her write um & therefore you must take the will for the deed. god bye. Your most loving obededunt faithfull & hunbel sarvant.[33]

Laurence would return after the treaty of Nijmegen was signed in August. In fact, several treaties were signed between August 1678 and October 1679 to create peace across Europe. The treaties ended various wars, but most importantly between France and the Dutch Republic. There would be no need for England to be involved in hostilities any more. Nell mentions she is for war but only to see her friend safely home.

Nell also comments on several people in this letter, one being Sir Carr Scrope, who Rochester coined the 'ugly beau-garcon', and who was another wit, a poet and writer. Nell had welcomed him to her home and he often visited, though perhaps a little too much. He fell in love with her and when Nell spurned him, he turned nasty. She mourned his loss as a friend not a lover.

She also talks of going to have supper with the King and Lady Harvey, but she was unaware of this woman's true motives. There was, in fact, a plot afoot to provide the King with a new mistress. Ralph Montagu, eager to be back in favour, was angling for a new position, that of Secretary of State, or Lord Treasurer should Danby be replaced. His sister, Lady

Elizabeth Harvey, the woman Nell refers to, felt there was no better way to get closer to Charles than by enticing him into an affair with Jane Middleton (a young girl who may have been Montagu's illegitimate daughter). Nell seems to have been oblivious to the undertones to this new friendship, but her companions saw the danger of Jane becoming Charles' mistress and usurping Nell.

Henry Savile still held Nell in much affection, although her thoughts that he might marry an heiress came to nothing. Like Rochester, he suffered greatly from syphilis and was trying various remedies including mercury. By the time he wrote to Rochester, concerned about her well-being, he had been taking it in large doses for the past six months, yet he saw the threat to Nell in Lady Harvey's plan and wanted her warned. He wrote to Rochester on 4 June 1678 of his concerns:

> Your friend and sometimes (especially now) mine, has a part in it that makes her now laughed att and may one day turn to her infinite disadvantage. This case stands thus if I am rightly informed: My Lady Hervey who allways loves one civill plot more, is working body and soule to bring Mrs Jenny Middleton into play. How dangerous a new one is to all old ones I need not tell you, but her Ladyship, having little opportunity of seeing Charlemagne upon her owne account, wheedles poor Mrs nelly into supper twice or thrice a week at W Cs (Chiffinch's) and carrying her with her; so that in good earnest this poor creature is betrayed by her Ladyship to pimp against herselfe; for there her Ladyship whispers and contrives all matters to her owne ends, as the other might easily perceive if she were not too giddy to mistrust a false friend[34]

Rochester, as Nell mentioned, was at his country seat. He knew Jane Middleton intimately and he asked Savile to caution Nell about what they were up to, counselling, 'My advice to the lady has ever been this, take your measures just contrary to your rivals, live in peace with the world, and easily with the King: Never be so illnatur'd to stir up his anger against others, but let him forget the use of a passion, which is never to do you good … Please him with body, head and heart.'[35] Rochester would always remain loyal to Nell although he loathed Barbara and

Louise. Nell must have taken their advice and no more is heard of Lady Harvey after her plot to make Jane Middleton one of the King's regular mistresses failed.

Nell had been too trusting in this case and she was no naïve young woman. Perhaps because Elizabeth Harvey was a lady, she felt she had good intentions. People often asked for Nell's help and she would always try to give it. She could be too kind-hearted for her own good. That summer the King's illegitimate son by Lucy Walter, the Duke of Monmouth, wanted her help to persuade the King to legitimise him. Charles had certainly considered it, but to legitimise Monmouth he would have to admit he had been married to his mother. Nell did her best to help the man she called 'Prince Perkin' in a nod to Perkin Warbeck (a pretender to the throne in Henry VII's reign who claimed to be Richard of Shrewsbury, Duke of York, the second son of Edward IV and one of the Princes in the Tower), but the king was adamant. He told her he would rather see his son hanged at Tyburn than have him succeed to the throne.

Nell must have been relieved to see out the rest of the summer at Windsor. She had gone ahead to prepare for the King's arrival, but he would be caught up for some days by something much more sinister than a plot to put a lady in his bed.

*****

On 13 August 1678 Charles, accompanied by his beloved spaniels, set out for a long stroll around St James's Park. His brother James had repeatedly asked him not to, worried he would be assassinated, but Charles just laughed and said no one would kill him to put James on the throne. On this day, Christopher Kirkby, an employee in the King's laboratory, approached him and implored him to seek safety as he was in immediate danger. The King took no notice and carried on, but it was only the beginning of what would become known as The Popish Plot – a supposed plot by Catholics to kill the King. Although the plot was pure invention, it would lead to three years of trouble. The fear it caused would trigger anti-Catholic attitudes, instigate the deaths of many blameless people and almost ruin the Queen.

Poor Catherine had not had an easy marriage to Charles, but she had come to accept their relationship contained more than the two of them.

Her biggest sorrow and regret was that she had not been able to have a child. Although she attended court functions, she lived away from the madness of Whitehall at Somerset House, where, as a practising Catholic, she had her own chapel.

Kirkby had truly believed that two men, Pickering and Grove, were going to assassinate the King, but when Danby conducted a private investigation into the matter and tried to find the men, he couldn't. Kirkby didn't know it but he had been played by Titus Oates, the main instigator of the plot who would draw many others into his scheming.

On 6 September Oates went to the magistrate, Sir Edmund Berry Godfrey, to swear the truth of his allegations, that the Catholics, some of them eminent courtiers, were planning to rise up and slaughter all the Protestants in England. The King would be killed and the Pope would give control of the country to the Jesuits. And to top it all, he said the Queen and her servants were at the heart of it. When Sir Edmund Berry Godfrey went missing and was found dead in a ditch at Primrose Hill, impaled on his own sword, it caused mass hysteria.

Charles could not and would not believe the Queen was involved. He knew just how much she had gone through and perhaps had reason to see him dead, nonetheless, he knew she would never countenance it. He asked her to return to her apartments in Whitehall so that she would be under his protection.

Oates formally accused Queen Catherine with conspiring with her physician to poison the King. Evelyn recorded that even though she must have feared for her life, the Queen still held her birthday celebrations. 'I never saw the court more brave, nor the nation in more apprehension and consternation ... Oates grew so presumptuous as to accuse the queen of a design to poison the king, which certainly that pious and virtuous lady abhorred the thoughts of, and Oates's circumstances made it utterly unlikely, in my opinion. He probably thought to gratify some who would have been glad his majesty should have married a fruitful lady; however, the king was too kind a husband to let any of these make impression on him.'[36]

Of course, his French mistress, Louise, was also Catholic. She might have hoped for the Queen's fall but seeing as she was of the same religion, her popularity, if she really ever had any, took a dive. Nell was the only Protestant among them.

The court returned to London on 16 October, but Nell and her son Charles went to Cambridge where she was welcomed by the vice-chancellor and presented with poetry written by some of the finest scholars. Nell had her own Pope-burning party on 5 November 1678 and invited all her friends. The Pope was set up by her front door and the local children spent the evening throwing bangers at it. After all the tumult of the Popish Plot, Nell made sure everyone knew exactly where her sympathies lay.

Chapter Seven

Loss and Love 1679-1681

The aftermath of the Popish Plot rumbled on. Investigations and trials continued and more than anything England swelled with anti-Catholic sentiment. The succession and the Duke of York's position as heir was a key issue. A bill to exclude Charles' brother because of his faith was introduced in May but the King dissolved Parliament before it could be passed. Concerned for James's safety, Charles sent him to Brussels, saying it was 'for my service and your own good.'[1] The people were much more in favour of the dashing Duke of Monmouth as the next heir to the throne, so obviously his father's son, but the King refused to agree and the succession remained unchanged. It was an issue that would be continually raised in Parliament over the next few years.

Monmouth was all the more popular for his recent military foray into Scotland and his victory at the battle of Bothwell Bridge. A rebellion by Covenanters in south-west Scotland was easily quashed by the young duke and his 5,000-strong army. He returned to London to a hero's welcome, the people waving and cheering as he rode through the streets to Whitehall. Yet behind his triumphant façade lay a troubled man. His friend James Welwood wrote of him: 'the first part of [Monmouth's] life was all Sunshine, though the rest was clouded. He was Brave, Generous, Affable, and extremely Handsome: Constant in his Friendships, just to his Word, and an utter Enemy to all sort of Cruelty. He was easy in his nature, and fond of popular Applause, which led him insensibly into all his misfortunes.'[2]

An early biographer tells of how his father was still unhappy with his son, especially since he had spared the lives of his prisoners. Charles is supposed to have said to Monmouth, 'If I had been there, we would not have had the trouble of prisoners,' to which Monmouth replied, 'I cannot kill men in cold blood, that's work only for butchers.'[3] Given that Charles had pursued his father's regicides and soon tired of their bloody executions, this story is unlikely. His friends who often should have faced the death penalty were let off and when the infamous Colonel Blood, who tried to steal the crown jewels, a treasonous act, was pardoned, it gave a clear signal that Charles did not deal in death.

The King's relationship with his son was fractious and would only worsen over the next few years. Charles thought he was grasping and stubborn, Monmouth thought Charles was cold and unyielding. The duke was on a downward spiral, although he did not yet know it and his father would not live to see it.

It was with some relief that the court left the city for the summer at Windsor, but Nell would have no time to enjoy the peaceful parks and the walks that Charles would spend time planning. On 20 July 1679 Nell's drunken mother, who had been sitting by a stream near her house in Chelsea, fell in and drowned. It seems that in 1676 she moved out of Nell's Pall Mall home to her own lodgings, possibly to Sandford Manor House. When Nell heard the news of her mother's demise she travelled from Windsor to London to arrange her funeral. Madame Gwyn was buried on 30 July 1679, around the age of fifty-six, at St Martin-in-the-Fields. Nell wanted to see her out in style and asked her friends Buckingham, Rochester, Buckhurst and Sedley to help out. They dressed as bishops to lead a mock extravagant procession to take Nell's mother to her final resting place. Her hearse was highly decorated with the blue lion of the Gwyns of Llansanor in pride of place and was followed by Nell and Rose in their coach. Nell's servants dressed in their finest livery and her friends turned out in their best clothes. The procession wound its way through the streets of London, past the Theatre Royal where more people from Nell's life, actors and bawds, joined the procession as it passed through Covent Garden and on to the church.

It was the talk of the town and there were many tributes to the woman who had raised Nell, however poorly, some more scathing than others. Madame Gwyn was a well-known figure and the satirists of the day had much to say about her.

> Her Mother griev'd in muddy Ale and Sack
> To think her Child should ever prove a Crack;
> When she was drunk she always fell asleep,
> And when full maudlin, then the whore would weep;
> Her tears were brandy, Mundungus her breath,

Bawd was her Life, and Common-shore her Death.
To see her Daughter mourn for such a Beast
Is like her Life, which makes up but one Jest.[4]

Rochester, also known for his wicked words, actually wrote one of the more pleasant tributes:

Nor was her Mother's Funeral less her care,
No cost, no velvet did the Daughter spare:
Five gulded 'Scutcheons did the Herse enrich,
To celebrate this Martyr of the Ditch.
Burnet Brandy did in flaming Brummers flow,
Drank at her funeral, while her well-leased Shade
Rejoyc'd, even in the sober Fields below,
At all the drunkenness her Death had made.[5]

After the funeral, free beer and brandy flowed in a tribute to Nell's mother. It was one send-off that wouldn't be forgotten in a hurry, but Nell had no time to mourn the woman who had raised her. The King had fallen seriously ill and she had to return to Windsor. Given the current climate, it was rumoured he had been poisoned. Savile wrote to Rochester fearing another civil war should he die. But despite the rumours, the King had just caught a chill after playing tennis and then going fishing along the banks of the Thames.

There is a lovely story that Nell stayed by his side every day and nursed him back to health and that the Queen gave special permission for Nell to attend him. Instead of his usual court physicians, she sent for two wise women she knew who had the best cures and together they nursed him back to health. In reality, Nell would have been kept away – she wasn't family or blood and had no place in the King's bedchamber when he was ill.

The Duke of York had been sent for, in case the King's illness proved fatal, but Charles rallied and recovered before the duke even arrived. James was packed off to Scotland this time and enjoyed staying there, indulging in hunting, hawking and other country pursuits. The fear of the King's demise was so great that Monmouth began agitating to be named his father's heir. When Charles heard that his son by Lucy Walter had been stirring the pot again he sent him to Holland. Nell's friend

Laurence Hyde reported that he was frantically writing letters to Nell to ask her to intervene with the King and let him return.

With Charles fully recovered, it was time to go to Newmarket as usual at the end of September. Nell enjoyed dressing up as a man in breeches and a periwig to impersonate one of the owners and walk around the stables. It harked back to her actress days. At that time the trend of cross-dressing was considered fashionable, though outrageous to some, Pepys included. He wrote in his diary: 'Walking here in the galleries at White Hall, I find the ladies of Honour dressed in their riding garbs, with coats and doublets with deep skirts, just for all the world like mine, and buttoned their doublets up the breast, with periwigs and with hats; so that, only for a long petticoat dragging under their men's coats, nobody could take them for women in any point whatever; which was an odd sight, and a sight, (which) did not please me.'[6]

Nell, however, was no accomplished horsewoman. In October she had a serious fall and her steward, Sir Fleetwood Sheppard, escorted her back to London. Sheppard was a friend of the King's and another one of the notorious Merry Gang, who 'after his majesty's Restoration ... retir'd to London, hang'd on the court, became a debauchee and atheist.'[7] He had known Nell for years and was also close to her former lover, Charles Buckhurst, Earl of Dorset, with whom he went on a trip to Paris that caused some scandal. He seems to have taken the position with Nell around the time she gave birth to her second son, which caused one satirist to call him the best paid pimp in the land.

The Duke of Grafton, Barbara and the King's second son, married Isabella, Lord Arlington's daughter, on 8 November and Nell attended. She had the money spare for a new dress, mostly owing to Sir Robert Howard, who, acting as her trustee, had liaised with the Duke of Ormond to see her finally receive revenue from her Irish estates in Dundalk and Carlingford. Nell asked Howard to write to the duke, 'Mrs Nelly presents you with her real acknowledgements for all your favours, and protests that she would write in her own hands, but her wild characters, she says, will distract you.'[8]

The extra funds were welcome as the King was trying to curtail his expenses. Due to no longer receiving a French pension, nor receiving funds through Parliament, cutbacks were necessary, but he still paid Nell's pension. A royal warrant issued earlier in June reaffirmed her position. 'Our will and pleasure is, And wee doe hereby Authorise and require you, Out of Our Treasure now or hereafter being or remaining in the Receipt of Our Exchequer, to pay or cause to be paid unto Eleanor Gwyn or her Assignes the Annuity or yearly Summe of Five thousand pounds, Dureing Our pleasure, for and towards the Support and maintenance of herselfe and Charles Earle of Burford, To be received by the said Eleanor Gwyn quarterly, Att the foure most usuall feasts in the yeare by equall porcions.'[9]

But the money never came quite on time or in large enough sums so Nell still found herself in debt and struggling to make ends meet. Another story about Nell has her asking the King for money. When he said he had none, Nell replied, 'I shall tell you how you shall: Send ye French into France again, sett me on the stage again and lock up your codpiece!' Louise managed better with her French subsidies and a grant from the King of estates forfeited by suicides and those who had been executed. Barbara, too, was still draining the exchequer dry and somehow managed to get £25,000 out of the treasury that autumn. Was Charles paying her off for a quiet life?

There were entertainments in November when Lord Shaftesbury, a constant agitator, put on an anti-Catholic pageant to mock 'the Pope, Cardinalls, Jesuits, Fryers, &c'[10] through the streets of London. Fearing it might get out of hand, Charles told Nell not to go, but she couldn't resist. She only wanted to see the actors in the procession and enjoy the evening. Nell missed the playhouse, though she was still remembered by writers such as Aphra Behn, who dedicated *The Feign'd Courtesans* to her, and Robert Whitcomb, who likened Nell to divine gods and goddesses in *Janna Divorum*, writing that she had the attributes of 'the primitive wisdom of Apollo, the pristine wit of Venus, and the God-like courage and brave spirit of Hercules.'[11]

At times there were those who rallied against Charles' mistresses. Nell's coachman was beaten up by some ruffians who called her a whore. He had defended her honour and paid for his loyalty. Nell told him he shouldn't have because it was true, to which he replied, 'That may be, madam, but I'll not be called a whore's coachman.' In another incident, Nell was driving in Hyde Park when her horse bumped into that of Lieutenant Wharton, who, in a rage, drew his sword and decided to kill the poor creature. Nell was horrified and told Charles what had happened. He immediately had the lieutenant sent to Holland.

Monmouth, the Protestant duke, who had continued to write to Nell, returned after a month without permission and hid at her house, which put her relationship with the King under strain. It seems that Charles was unaware she was hiding him, and when he visited, Monmouth was 'shut up in her closet.'[12] She tried to mediate between them but Charles was furious with his errant son and would not listen to her pleas. 'Nelly dus the Duck of Monmouth all the kindness she can, but her interest is nothing. Nell Gwin begg'd hard of his majestie to see him, that he was grown wan, lean and long visage merely because he was in disfavour; but the King bid her be quiet for he wd not see him.'[13] Nell had tried her best but when Monmouth told her that he still wanted his place in the succession, she had to ask him to leave. Their situation was captured in a satire.

> True to the Protestant Interest and cause,
> True to th'establish'd Government and Laws,
> The Chief delight of the whole Mobile (rabble),
> Scarce Monmouth's self is more belov'd than shee.
> Was this the cause that did their quarrel move,
> That both are Rivalls in the Peoples Love?
> No, twas her Matchless loyaltie alone
> That bid prince Perkin pack up and be gone.[14]

Buckingham was also staying with Nell and planning to provide the King with another mistress to replace Louise. Her home at 79 Pall Mall was fast becoming a place for intrigue. This time he had fixed on Jane Lawson, one of his sister's nieces, and it seems that the Duchess of Richmond (his sister), Lady Mary Howard (her aunt), Nell and Laurence Hyde were in on the plan. For Nell of course it would be a way to trump her rival, Louise, but giving the King another mistress was not without its perils. Another satire published at the time warned Jane Lawson not to get involved.

> O yet consider e're it be too late
> How near you stand upon the brink of fate.
> Think who they are who would for you procure
> This great preferment to be made a whore:
> Two reverend aunts, renowned in British story

> For lust and drunkenness with Nell and Lory.
> These, these are they your fame will sacrifice,
> Your honour sell, and you shall hear the price:
> My Lady Mary nothing can design,
> But to feed her lust with what she gets for thine;
> Old Richmond making thee a glorious punk,
> Shall twice a day with brandy now be drunk;
> Her brother Buckingham shall be restored;
> Nelly a countess, Lory be a lord.[15]

This was yet another plot that came to nothing, and Jane Lawson went to live in a convent. The King had settled down, it seems, content enough with the mistresses he had.

There were strange rumours about Nell that December, that she hadn't been seen or heard and had most likely been killed by Jesuits. She was, of course, in perfect health and preparing for the celebrations over Christmas. Her friend John Dryden, however, was beaten up for mistakenly being the author of a satire that attacked those most notable at court. Rochester was blamed for Dryden's injuries although other stories suggested that Louise had got her vicious and violent brother-in-law, the Earl of Pembroke, to do the deed. Given that their relationship was an extremely unpleasant one, if Pembroke was involved it would not have been at her behest. The culprit went undetected and it would later be revealed that the real author of the satire was Lord Mulgrave.

Nell started the year delighted with a gift from Charles of the newly built Burford House in Windsor next to the royal park. Colonel Whichcote had bought the land, once used as a garden or vineyard, to the south of the castle but it came into Charles' possession after his restoration. He used the land to build a new tennis court and Burford House. Antonio Verrio, the Italian painter, who had been employed to decorate the north range of the castle, which included the King's Chapel and St George's Hall, twenty ceilings and three staircases, for a massive £10195 8s 4d, also decorated Nell's staircase with stories from Ovid at a cost of £100. Grinling Gibbons, who was also working on the north range, created a chimneypiece in an upstairs room. The house sat in its own ornamental gardens and Nell even had her own orangery. It would become a wonderful retreat as she would never be far from the King on their trips to Windsor.

In January 1680 Nell's old friend, and possibly lover, Charles Sedley, who had stayed with her and Buckhurst in Epsom, was seriously injured. Stories say it was when his play *Bellamira*, which was atrocious, was being performed, but it seems that the dates are out as the production was not launched until 1687. 'It was the Acting of his Play call'd Bellamira, that the Roof of the Playhouse fell down. But what was particular, was that very few were hurt but himself. His merry friend Sir Fleetwood Shepherd told him, There was so much fire in his Play that it blew up the Poet, House, and all. He told him again, NO: the play was so Heavy that it broked down the House, and buried the Poet in his own rubbish.'[16]

The stories of what happened were embellished by the wits and rakes of the age, and these grew in the telling. What is certain is that some roof, somewhere – a tennis court was also mentioned – did fall on Sedley, and his head injuries were so bad he was thought not to survive. Sir George Etherege was also badly wounded. It would be some time before Sedley recovered and it was said he was a new man when he did, giving up his debauched, errant ways and turning to God.

> Sidley the Bold, the witty and the gay,
> Whose tongue has lead so many Maids a stray
> Has laid aside the Vices of the Lay,
> And in the Arms of Mother Church at last
> More than attones for All his wandrings past[17]

Whether Nell believed he had truly found God or not we don't know, but he would outlive a lot of the Merry Gang. He also turned to politics, which kept him busy up until his death in 1701.

Nell too was in an incident that spring when she attended the Duke's theatre with George Herbert, the younger brother of the Earl of Pembroke, who must have been nothing like his sibling. A drunkard called out, 'Nelly's horse is dead, but Nell the whore is here,' referring to the incident in Hyde Park with Lieutenant Wharton. Her companion leapt down into the pit, brandishing his sword, intent on avenging the insult until Nell calmed him down. Nevertheless, the gathered crowd thought it was hilarious, and, grabbing the drunkard, deposited him outside in a horse trough.

In April 1680 the subject of Monmouth's legitimacy reared its ugly head again. Charles once more declared he had never married Lucy

Walter, the Duke of Monmouth's mother. But some people believed he had and that there was a marriage contract. This marriage contract was supposed to have been given to Bishop John Cosin before Lucy's death, securely sealed into a black box. The box was then believed to have come into the possession of Sir Gilbert Gerard, Cosin's son-in-law. The Privy Council had to investigate this claim and called Gerard to an extraordinary meeting for questioning, but he denied all knowledge of the marriage contract or ever having a black box in his keeping. Charles was heartily sick of the subject, but this at last would see the matter put to rest.

Nell became ill in May. Although we can't be certain what her illness was, some of her biographers have speculated she was suffering from syphilis and keeping it quiet. She stayed at home for many weeks and worse was to come. When news came of her youngest son James's death of a 'poor leg' in Paris, she was utterly devastated. There had been no indication that he was ill, although, looking at the apothecary bills, he was not as strong and healthy in his youth as his brother. We don't know what happened – an accident, illness or infected wound – and his time in France remains a mystery. Even where he is buried is not known. If he had been interred in England there would have been a record of it, so his body never returned home and Nell had no way to say her final goodbyes.

In her misery, Nell swore that Louise had had him poisoned. Her grief was such that the King had to try to calm and console her, urging her to move on and focus on her new house in Windsor. In time she would turn to redecorating and making the house a meeting place for her theatrical friends, writers like Edmund Waller and Aphra Behn, who described Nell as gladding 'the hearts of all that have the happy fortune to see you,'[18] and entertaining rich nobles like Monmouth and Buckingham.

But where she mourned has been debated. One biographer suggests she stayed at Sandford Manor House in Fulham. It seems that this is another part of London that claims a connection to Nell. An account written in the Victorian era tells of how the writer tried to find out more about the house and met with an old man, the local rat catcher, who explained:

Nell Gwynne's house at Sandy End, where runs the little river they deepened into a canal – the stream I mean that

divides Chelsea from Fulham – Sandford manor House!
… It must have been a pleasant place in those days, when
the king was making his private road through the Chelsea
fields, and the stream was as clear as a thrush's eye and birds
of all sorts were so tamed by Madam Ellen, that they'd come
when she called them. Ah, a pretty woman might catch a
king, but it's only a kind one that could tame the wild birds
of the air.'[19]

An edition of *The Gentleman's Magazine* contains an article that tells
how 'the rooms rang with her merry peals of laughter,' and in the
garden 'her good angel came to her and taught her to work out some
practical scheme for the comfort of the poor and afflicted',[20] presumably
referencing her charitable endeavours. Apparently a thimble engraved
with her initials N.G. upon it was found in the house, but as we know
from her letters and silverware, she actually used E.G. A jewel of Charles'
was also understood to have been discovered under the floorboards and
it was said the trees in the garden were planted by his own hand. Of
course there was a secret recess – although not a tunnel – and to top it
all the King was supposed to have ridden up the staircase on his horse!
In 1971 the house's restoration came under debate in the House of Lords
as the 'reputed' house of Nell Gwyn. Lord Sandford at the time stated
he knew of no connection to his family 'or, indeed, with the lady named
in the Question.'[21]

As always stories associating Nell with a house or area are as colourful
as she was. There is absolutely no evidence she was at Sandford Manor
House, but it could have been used for parties, rented for liaisons with
the King or used as a summer house. This, seemingly, was the case with
Bagnigge House on the King's Cross Road, near Clerkenwell in London.
Here Nell 'entertained Charles and his saturnine brother with concerts
and merry breakfasts in the careless bohemian way in which the noble
specimen of divine right delighted.'[22] It was the site of two wells that
were opened to the public as a spa retreat in 1760. But again the evidence
for Nell living at this property is slight.

Wherever Nell mourned her son, she was in desperate pain, in a dark
and painful place. Charles did his best to comfort her but he was never
very good at dealing with emotions. It would be a while before Nell
absorbed herself in the work at Burford House, but she would rise from

her grief, put a smile back on her face and become once more the woman who made the King smile at her antics.

The people had all the sympathy in the world for Nell. Louise, however, was another matter. Louise was not in a happy place yet we can be fairly certain she did not consider poisoning Nell's son. With the aftermath of the Popish Plot still discernible, the King's French mistress became a target. She had surpassed even Barbara in draining the treasury dry and her yearly pension was now in the region of £17,000. In the past three years her secret service payments amounted to over £4 million in today's money, whereas Nell only received approximately a third of that. The Venetian ambassador reported, 'The more politically minded dwell upon the quantity of gold which the King has given and which he lavishes daily upon his favoured lady, who is a Frenchwoman.'[23] Hatred for her ran rife. She was vilified in numerous publications including this poem.

> Portsmouth, that pocky bitch,
> A damned papistical drab,
> An ugly, deformed witch,
> Eaten up with the mange and scab.
> This French hag's pocky bum
> So powerful is of late,
> Although it's blind and dumb,
> It rules both Church and State.[24]

She began making plans to leave for France should her situation become too dangerous. A pamphlet entitled *Articles of High Treason and Other High Crimes and Misdemeanours against the Duchess of Portsmouth* was published which listed her faults and supposed crimes. In the summer Shaftesbury and seven supporting lords indicted the Duke of York for being a Popish recusant. The case was dismissed but he also claimed that Louise was a 'national nuisance' and was nothing more than a common prostitute. Louise knew her days were numbered.

For Nell, there was more sorrow to come. Her dear and loyal friend, and notorious hell-raiser and rake, the Earl of Rochester died on 26 July and was buried at Spelsbury church in Oxfordshire. He was only thirty-three but his body was riddled with syphilis and the effects of alcohol misuse. Burnet described him as being 'Like a comet, he flashed across the stormy night of the seventeenth century, filling those who knew him with astonishment, leaving behind a memory that faded after many years.'[25] To Nell those memories were still fresh and she would always carry him in her heart.

Mourning her losses, Nell moved to Burford House to grieve and remember sunnier days. She filled her time with redecorating and caring for her eldest son, employing a new tutor for him. Nell chose Thomas Otway, an actor and poet, but he was another man too friendly with her maids, and when he got one pregnant she had to let him go. She returned to London in September for a brief visit to witness the conveyance of her house deeds, and then moved on to Newmarket for the races. Sir John Reresby gives a snapshot of the King at one of his favourite towns: 'The manner of the king's dividing his time at this place was this he walked in the morning till ten of the clock; then he went to the Cock Pit till dinner time; about three he went to the horse races; at six he returned to the Cock Pit, for an hour only; then he went to the play, though the actors were but of a terrible sort; from thence to supper; then to the Duchess of Portsmouth's till bedtime; and so on to his own apartment to take his rest.'[26]

He doesn't mention Nell, though she was always at Newmarket with the King, except in 1679 when their son was ill with distemper. She was a permanent fixture in the King's daily routine but perhaps he thought her too inconsequential to mention. Charles took his duties as a father seriously and arranged a day trip to Portsmouth with their son to see the launch of the warship named after him, *The Burford*.

There was yet another death in December, this time of the famous painter Lely who had captured Nell and Charles so well. On 12 December Evelyn wrote, 'I saw a meteor of an obscure bright colour, very much in shape like the blade of a sword ... what this may portend God only knows.'[27] Nell must have been wondering the same thing. The passing year had worn her down and even she, the wittiest, most charming and cheerful of people, was struggling to put on a brave face.

The King had had ongoing troubles with Parliament and especially Lord Shaftesbury, a seasoned soldier who had fought on both Royalist and Parliamentary sides in the civil war. He had served as Chancellor of the Exchequer in 1661, and in 1672 he was promoted to Lord Chancellor, but he was an agitator and supporter of Monmouth's claim to the succession. He disliked the Queen and felt she should be replaced with a strong Protestant woman. He wanted Catherine removed from the throne 'as the sole remaining chance of security, liberty and religion'. He thought 'a bill of divorce might pass, which, by separating the King from Queen Catherine, might enable him to marry a Protestant consort, and thus leave the crown to legitimate issue.'[28] The King, ever loyal to his women, would hear none of it.

Edward Fitzharris, employed by the Duchess of Portsmouth, published a pamphlet, *A True Englishman Speaking Plain English in a Letter from a Friend to a Friend,* which brought the succession into question again and libelled both the King and his brother. Fitzharris also claimed that he had been told that the Queen was plotting to poison her husband.

In March 1681 Parliament was to be held at Oxford – a Royalist stronghold during the war – even though Shaftesbury tried petitioning for it to be held at Whitehall as normal. He wanted the whole issue of the succession, the Queen and Fitzharris' claims to be addressed. He insisted that the Duke of Monmouth be declared legitimate. It was not going to be a pleasant meeting.

Charles and Catherine left the city for Oxford on 14 March 1681 under a cloud of trepidation. Louise and Nell followed on in separate coaches. Unfortunately, Nell's coach was mistaken for Louise's and she had to shout out to the crowd 'Pray, good people, be civil. I am the Protestant whore!'

On 26 March 1681 Shaftesbury brought up the Exclusion Bill again and Charles swiftly dissolved Parliament. It would be the last of his reign. Two parliaments had been dissolved and the King issued a *Declaration to All His Loving Subjects* by way of explanation. It was to be read out in churches and copies distributed. The public needed to know about the 'malice of ill men who are labouring to poison our people.'[29] It was damage limitation, but for Charles, Shaftesbury was an evil element and one that needed to be contained. On 2 July 1681 he was arrested for high treason and committed to the Tower of London in rooms next to Danby. Shaftesbury would be released the following year, but Danby, who had been implicated in the Popish Plot and the murder of Sir Edmund Berry Godfrey, would stay in the Tower until 1684.

Nell's responsibility throughout all of Charles' political woes was to be his sounding board, his comfort and his shoulder to lean on. She understood far more than people gave her credit for and was also grateful that, unlike the Queen and Louise, her reputation went unscathed.

The King was grateful for her love and support and, in time-honoured fashion, gave her a gift. In April 1681 Charles granted Nell the leasehold of Bestwood Lodge, a former hunting lodge in Sherwood Forest near Nottingham. Knowing that she was so bad at riding, Charles had promised her as much of the forest as she could ride around before breakfast. Nell was not an early riser and the King's guess was she wouldn't be up long enough to get much riding in. The next morning, however, she woke early and rode merrily around the boundary, dropping handkerchiefs to mark out her territory, before she triumphantly had breakfast with the King.

Apart from her house in Pall Mall, Burford House was her favourite property. Nell was at Windsor in the summer when her old friend John Dryden visited her and the King to read them the first part of his satirical poem, *Absalom and Achitopel*, a reworking of the Biblical tale of Absalom's rebellion against King David, his father. Dryden, through the use of satire and allegory, represented Absalom as Monmouth, Achitopel as Shaftesbury and Charles as King David, and touched on the Exclusion Crisis and the Popish Plot.

In June, Edward Fitzharris was charged with high treason for his seditious pamphlet. Louise was called as a witness. She was absolutely horrified at having to take part in such a degrading situation and told the jury, 'I have nothing at all to say to Mr Fitzharris, nor was concerned in any sort of business with him. All I have to say is he desired me to give a petition to the King to get his estate in Ireland, and I did three or four times speak to the King about it. But I have not anything else to say to him.' After more evidence was given, Louise did find something to say to the guilty man. 'Mr Fitzharris, if I had anything in the world to do you good, I would do it; but I have not, and so can't see that I am any ways more useful here.'[30] With that she left the court. Fitzharris was sentenced to hang at Tyburn and Louise was left shamefaced at the whole affair.

A satire published this year, *A Pleasant Battle between two lap dogs of the utopia court – Tutty & Snap-short*, imagined the conversation between Nell's and Louise's dogs.

> The English lap-dog here does first begin
> The vindication of his lady, Gwynn:
> The other, much more Frenchified, alas,
> Shows what his lady is, not what she was.[31]

The dogs discuss the merits of their mistresses with Snap-short calling Nell an 'open-arse lady, who came lately from selling oranges and lemmons about the streets.' A fight is about to ensue when Nell and Louise sweep into the room to break them up and Nell tells her:

> Pray, Madam, stand a little farther, as you respect your own flesh, for my little dog is mettle to the back, and smells a Popish Miss at a far greater distance: pray, Madam, take warning, for you stand on dangerous ground.[32]

Nell would not be sorry to see Louise return to her home country but there was no sign of her leaving just yet.

Nell's old friend John Lacy died in September 1681. It was such a terrible year for loss. His passing made her reminisce about the old days. She was young still but her acting days were fast becoming a distant memory. The theatre she had loved so much had changed almost beyond recognition. Tom Killigrew had retired in 1677 and his sons, Charles and the dissolute Harry, took over the theatre, but it had run into trouble. It wouldn't be long until the King's Company and the Duke's Company would merge to become the United Company, managed by Thomas Betterton.

Even so, several of the actresses had landed on their feet and found rich men to look after them. In 1671 Peg Hughes gave birth to Prince Rupert's daughter, Ruperta. Although Rupert was urged to return to the Palatinate, marry and produce an heir, he remained with Peg who had continued acting with the Duke's Company until 1677. Nell was delighted for her friend when the prince bought her the impressive Brandenburgh House in Hammersmith, joining them both at dinners in London, Newmarket and Windsor. Their friendship nearly turned sour when Peg's brother was killed in 'a dispute whether Mrs Nelly or she (his sister) was the handsomer now at Windsor.'[33] But they had remained friends and Rupert had at one point hoped that Ruperta would marry Nell's son Charles. He delighted in his daughter, who ruled 'the whole house and sometimes argues with her mother, which makes us all laugh,' but the marriage never went ahead. In fact, Charles Beauclerk would not marry until much later in life.

Nell's altruistic side is told in one story where a one-legged man stopped her coach, begging for money. This encounter made her think of the homeless civil war veterans who were not looked after and ended up on the streets, men she saw on her daily trips around the city. This particular man had served in Tangier in North Africa, given to the Crown in the Queen's dowry, and had had his leg shot off. When she mentioned his plight to Charles it inspired him to establish a 'Committee for the Building of an hospital or infirmary for souldiers', which would become the Royal Hospital Chelsea, home of the Chelsea Pensioners. Of course, we don't know for sure that Nell instigated its building, but she was with Charles when Christopher Wren showed them preliminary sketches of the building and is supposed to have given over some extra land for them to build on, tearing up a handkerchief in four pieces and laying it over the plans to show it should be much bigger.

The infamous Samuel Pepys, who by now had given up writing his diary due to his failing eyesight, is also supposed to have supported the venture after Nell discussed it with him. An early biographer suggests Pepys and Nell became firm friends in his later years and that he often stayed with Nell at Oxford and Pall Mall, but it is more likely that he saw her on his visits to the King. Whether true or not, Nell is still associated with the hospital to this day.

Chapter Eight

Death of a King 1682-1685

JANUARY began with a visit from the Moroccan ambassador, Nahed Achmet, and his beautifully dressed, scimitar-carrying entourage to discuss the situation in Tangier, which had been fortified with English troops who found themselves under constant attack. The King and Queen held a banquet at Whitehall, which Nell attended, while Louise organised the entertainment. She was doing everything she could to please the King after the debacle of the Fitzharris affair. Evelyn wrote in his diary:

> This evening, I was at the entertainment of the Morocco Ambassador at the Duchess of Portsmouth's glorious apartments at Whitehall, where was a great banquet of sweetmeats and music, but at which both the Ambassador and his retinue behaved themselves with extraordinary moderation and modesty, though placed about a long table, a lady between two Moors, and among these were the King's natural children, namely, Lady Lichfield and Sussex, the Duchess of Portsmouth, Nelly, etc., concubines, and cattle of that sort, as splendid as jewels and excess of bravery could make them; the Moors neither admiring nor seeming to regard anything, furniture or the like, with any earnestness, and but decently tasting of the banquet.[1]

Gifts were exchanged and to everyone's amazement the ambassador brought with him two lions and thirty ostriches. It was rumoured that Louise was so enthralled with the swarthy, handsome stranger, she put her bid to return to favour to one side and took him to her bed.

It may have been why she decided to go to France in March when Charles went to Newmarket with Nell. Louise had grown a little plump and was unable to keep up with their hunting and hawking, besides which she had never really liked countryside pursuits. In France she was treated as a Queen and so stayed for two months, being fêted and revelling in her glorified status. Where once she had just been a maid of honour, now she commanded attention as the English king's mistress. There was no stigma attached to her position, quite the opposite. Louis XIV fully supported her and was also a king who could never stay faithful to his queen. But there was a more poignant side to her visit when she returned to Saint Cloud, where she had spent so much time with Charles' sister, Minette.

The King had not had time to miss Louise as he was busy with his civic duties, including laying the foundation stone for the Royal Hospital at Chelsea and touching his people for evil. Between May 1682 and April 1683 he would attempt to cure over 8,500 people. But he was also feeling his age and often put his feet up and slept at Nell's in the afternoon. In May he had a fit of the ague but recovered in time to welcome ambassadors from East India.

Dryden visited them again when they went to Windsor in the summer with the second part of his play. Burford House was a popular haunt for old friends and new, and Nell kept up her supper parties and evening entertainments. This year she invited her friend Mary Knight to stay and they got up to mischief, flirting with young officers of the guards, dramatised in 'Madame Nelly's Complaint', a satire that has Nell being haunted by her friend for stealing her lover, William Colt, Prince Rupert's Gentleman of the Horse and no doubt they shared an innocent flirtation, but Nell would never risk her relationship with the King.

Louise was back in July, fresh from her wonderful trip abroad and ready to dazzle the court with stories of her travels. As the saying goes absence makes the heart grow fonder and Charles was once more enamoured of his French mistress. Nell wasn't overly worried. She knew the fuss over Louise would soon die down, but one satire ran:

> Now Nelly you must be content,
> Her grace begins to reign;
> For all your brat you may be sent
> To Dorset (Buckhurst) back again.[2]

In August Nell accompanied Charles to Winchester where Christopher Wren was building him a new palace next to the old castle. Tired of city life, the King hoped to have a palace to rival that at Versailles, somewhere he could escape to away from all the chaos of Whitehall. The plans were on a grand scale, with 160 rooms, a staircase with marble columns and a cupola. Wren also designed the gardens and park to surround the palace, complete with a road that would lead straight to Winchester Cathedral.

All the fun of the summer, however, had left Nell severely short of money. Entertaining was a costly business and when Nell had money, she spent it. In September she had to write to the Duke of Ormond:

> This is to beg a favour of Your Grace, which I hope you will stand by my friend in. I lately got a friend of mine to advance me on my Irish pension half a year's payment for last Lady Day, which all people have received but me, and I drew bills upon Mr Laurence Steele, my agent, for the payment of the money, not thinking but that before this the bills had been paid; but contrary to my expectation I last night received advice from him that the bills are protested, and he cannot receive any money from Your Grace's positive order to the farmers for it. Your Grace formerly upon the King's letter, which this enclosed is the copy of, was so much mine and Mrs Forster's friend as to give necessary orders for our payments notwithstanding the stop. I hope you will oblige me now upon this request, to give your directions to the farmers, that we may be paid our arrears and what is growing due.[3]

Even though she had financial woes, Nell was always ready to help others. When the King was presented with a petition to aid the homeless of the great fire at Wapping she added £100 to Charles' £2,000.

Prince Rupert of the Rhine died from pleurisy on 29 November 1682 at his home in London, and after his state funeral was buried in Westminster Abbey. He left everything to his mistress, Peg Hughes, and his daughter, Ruperta. Peg decided to sell off some of his goods. To Nell, she offered a pearl necklace worth around £4,000 and Nell had to ask the King to buy it for her. She had never asked for much – unlike the other mistresses – and he was happy to help out.

The King was in an especially good mood in January when he heard that Shaftesbury, his parliamentary nemesis had died. Shaftesbury had fled to Amsterdam but had been continually unwell. A death that meant more to Nell was that of her old employer, Thomas Killigrew, who passed away in March at the age of seventy-one. The King paid £50 towards his funeral expenses and he was laid to rest next to Ben Jonson in Westminster Abbey. Harry, as his heir, was the main beneficiary of his will.

She nearly lost Charles that year when there was a plot or two to assassinate him. In January Sir Leoline Jenkins received an anonymous letter that read: 'Today, as the King went through the Park in his sedan from Mistress Gween's to Whitehall, two men were observed in disguise, whispering near the garden wall between the Pall Mall and the garden wall and I heard them say, Damn him, we shall never have such an occasion again. Prevent any evil that may happen, if neglected, or we three, that were witnesses and are known in the world, will call you to an account.'[4]

Charles' movements were regular and methodical and it would be easy to know where he was and when. His insistence on being available to his subjects also made him an easy target. The first plot this year was the prelude to something much more serious. As usual the King went off to Newmarket, but while there a fire destroyed some of the palace and other buildings in the town. Charles and James returned to Whitehall earlier than usual, not knowing that this had saved their lives. Rye House, near Hoddesdon, Hertfordshire, was on the road from Newmarket to London. Captain Richard Rumbold and a group of one hundred armed men planned to ambush the King and his brother on the way back from the races and kill them in cold blood. But the timing was off and the rebels were thwarted by the King's return three days early.

When the King found out, those responsible were sent to the Tower and hanged, drawn and quartered. There was one plotter, however, who escaped abroad and his involvement shocked the King to his core. It was his son, Monmouth. He would later confess his guilt but then retracted it when he returned home. Charles sent him into exile, saying he hoped he would go 'to Hell or Holland.'[5] He would never see him again.

Nell headed to Windsor for the summer with the King. Nothing she could say now would help Charles' eldest son. Her house was still a hub of activity and so she extended her lands, had walks put in around the gardens and added a bowling alley. These were precious days with Charles when the two of them could just relax in each other's company, have close friends to visit and see their son.

Nell's old lover, Charles Hart, had sold his shares in the King's Company, and due to a failing career and poor health, had retired in 1682 on a pension of 40 shillings per week. His affair with Barbara was long over. On 18 August he died and was buried at Great Stanmore, Middlesex. *An elegy on that worthy and famous actor, Mr. Charles Hart, who departed this life Thursday August the 18th. 1683* made much of his acting career and Nell would have agreed with the words:

> His Life the Stage instructed, and now dead,
> We're taught by Him the Worlds gay Stage to tread.
> Oh happy me! in such a Time brought forth,
> As to behold such Goodness, and such Worth.
> All that was Excellent we in Him might see,
> Servant to Justice, and strict Honesty:
> So Pure each Scene of's Life was, scarce we can
> Find Vice enough, to say He was but Man.
> His unexampl'd Virtues have no end,
> He was a Loyal Subject, Faithful Friend[6]

Someone who was not so faithful and now fell shockingly out of favour was Louise. During the summer, she fell in love with Hortense's nephew, Philippe de Vendome, Grand Prior of France, who came to England. He was young, handsome and showered Louise with attention. Attention that she had so long had to share with others. He made her feel young and alive. She knew she was aging and her figure was not what it used to be and here was a man who made her feel special. She took him to her bed and spoiled him with gifts. Of course, Charles was going to find out, and when he did he banished him, writing to Louis XIV to complain of his behaviour. If he had not tired of Louise by now, this affair certainly settled his relationship with her. She would go back to France for a time. On her return to England they would remain friends, but the passion had gone.

Charles must have despaired at the drama his mistresses brought with them at times. Nell was his constant, his comfort, his reprieve. She rarely troubled him as the others did. Yet he had to laugh when Hortense, whose current lover was killed in a duel, said she'd become a nun. That, he knew, would never happen.

Nell was there to keep him warm during that winter, the winter of the great freeze. The Thames was a solid block of ice for two months, in some places a foot deep. Charles had a pavilion set up where he and Nell could invite their friends and enjoy the Frost Fair entertainments of puppet shows, ice skating, bowling, sledging and football. Evelyn described the excitement: 'Coaches plied from Westminster to the Temple, and from several other stairs to and fro, as in the streets; sleds, sliding with skates, a bull-baiting, horse and coach races, puppet plays and interludes, cooks, tippling and other lewd places, so that it seemed to be a bacchanalian triumph, or carnival on the water.'[7]

It was a holiday on ice and one that Nell thoroughly enjoyed, taking her son to be with his father. In the New Year, Henry Jermyn, Earl of St Albans, once said to have secretly married the King's mother, died, leaving the title free for the King to make his son the Duke of St Albans, a title that came with additional lodgings in Whitehall and £1,500 a year. It would be the last creation of a title in Charles' reign. Nell had waited a long time for her son's ennoblement and she was absolutely delighted, showering the King with kisses and enthusiastically planning a superb party in celebration.

The diarist John Aubrey sent the new duke a copy of his findings regarding Avebury stone circle and for Nell there was a copy of *The Idea of the Education of a Young Gentleman*. As tutors went, young Charles had had a few. One Mr Clare had been with them for three years when she wrote to the Duke of Ormond to try to get him a command in the army: 'I forgot yesterday to speak to you about Mr Clare which makes me now trouble you with this letter, praying your Grace to give him some command in the army of Ireland. I have spoke to the King for him and the King said he would speak to your Grace, but least he might forget it, he bad me do it.'[8]

She also mentioned in the letter that Mr Clare would not be needed as her son was about to go to France. The letter has been dated 1684 but Charles had already spent two years in France under the care of Lord Preston, the English ambassador in Paris. A letter from George Legge to Preston shows how much the King cared for his son:

His Majesty is extremely fond of my Lord Burforde, and seems much concerned in his education, and he being now of an age fit to be bred in the world hath resolved to trust him wholly in your hands; no impertinent body shall be troublesome to you, not anybody but whom you approve of to wait on him. I am to be your solicitor providing money and all things necessary for him … I told his Majesty you would be forced to take a larger house and your expense must needs be much increased by this; he acknowledged it and bid me take care that my Lord Burforde should have an appointment ready provided by you in your own house … masters must be provided for him, the best can be got of all sorts, but most particularly the King would have him study mathematics, and in that fortification, and that when the King of France moves in any progresses he constantly go with you to view all places in France.[9]

St Albans had returned for Christmas 1683. It's possible that with his elevation, it was then decided he should stay at home and at court as he did not return to France.

Three leases for land and properties were signed by Nell with her 'E.G.' mark on 11 December 1684 to enlarge her holdings near Burford House in Windsor. Nell leased a house and stables on Priest Street and some land 'in a place there called the Old Hawes between the King's garden there on the north part, and the garden of sundry persons on the west and south parts and the little park of Windsor.'[10] The Dean and Canons of St George's Chapel also leased a garden in New Windsor to her at a cost of 12 shillings annual rent.

Charles must have footed the bill for the leases or thought to buy the properties outright as Nell was again short of ready cash and had to mortgage Bestwood Lodge. Sir John Musters forwarded her £3,000 and she was still writing to the Duke of Ormond to make sure her revenues came through. But yet again her lack of money did not stop her from helping others and when Dr Tenison, the vicar of her church in London, St Martin-in-the-Fields asked her to help out Huguenot refugees, she went to Charles and asked him for a purse of coin to give the vicar.

Yet she couldn't stop herself from buying when she saw something she really wanted. Lady Williams, one of the Duke of York's former mistresses, was selling some of her goods and Nell wanted them. She wrote to Madame Jennings, a seamstress, to talk to her about the 'gold stuff', but the letter is also a chaotic mix of need, gossip and enquiry. It is the longest letter we have of Nell's and as so few survive it is included in its entirety.

Madam – I have received your letter, and I desire you would speak to my Lady Williams to send me the gold stuff and a note with it, because I must sign it, ye next day of Mr Trant; pray tell her ladyship that I will send her a note of what quantity of things I'll have bought, if her ladyship will put herself to ye trouble to putt them; when they are bought I will sign a note for her to be paid. Pray, Madam, let ye man go on with my sedan, and sent Potevine and Mr Coker down to me for I want them both. The bill is very dear to boil the plate but necessity hath no law.

I am afraid Madam you have forgotten my mantle, which you were to line with musk colour satin, and all my other things, for you send me no patterns nor answer. Monsieur Lainey is going away. Pray send me word about your son Griffin, for His Majesty is mighty well pleased that he will go along with my Lord Duke. I am afraid you are so much taken up with your house that you forget my business. My service to dear Lord Kildare, and tell him I love him with all my heart. Pray, Madam, see that Potevine brings now all my things with him; my Lord Duke's bed etc. if he hath not made them all up, he may do that here, for if I do not get my things out of his hands now, I shall not have them until this time twelvemonth.

The Duke brought me down with him my crochet of diamonds; and I love it the better because he brought it. Mr Lumley and everybody else will tell you that it is the finest thing that ever was seen. Good madam, speak to Mr Beaver to come down too, that I may bespeak a ring for the Duke of Grafton before he goes into France.

I have continued extreme ill ever since you left me, and I am so still. I have sent to London for a doctor. I believe I shall die. My service to the Duchess of Norfolk, and tell her, I am as sick as her grace, but do not know what I ail, although she does, which I am overjoyed that she does with her great belly.

Pray tell my Lady Williams that the King's mistresses are accounted ill paymasters, but she shall have her money the next day after I have the stuff.

Here is a sad slaughter at Windsor, the young men taking
leaves and going to France, and although they are none of
my lovers, yet I am loath to part with the men. Mrs Jennings,
I love you will all my heart and so goodbye![11]

The summer was filled with their usual trip to Newmarket then on
to Windsor, but this year they also went to Winchester to see how the
King's new palace was coming along. It was there that Nell came up
against the royal chaplain, Thomas Ken, who had been asked to give her
accommodation during her stay. His response was, 'A woman of ill repute
ought not to be endured in the house of a clergyman, least of all in that of the
King's Chaplain.'[12] It was a stinging rebuke and one that Nell rarely heard
these days as she was so well accepted and loved. Apparently Ken had the
roof taken off his house so she couldn't be forced upon him. The Dean
had to have an extension built on the deanery for her but that ended up too
damp so Nell stayed at Avington with the Countess of Shrewsbury who
had spent some time in a French convent after her affair with Buckingham
and had remarried one George Bridges in 1677.

Charles had aged over the past months and the New Year saw in a
man who was near the end of his time and a King who was near the end
of his reign. His customary strolls had shortened and when he developed
an ulcer on his leg it put paid to his walks in the park. He stayed indoors
with his mistresses and Queen for company. His children often visited
him, to his delight. His family – albeit an unusual one – surrounded him
daily and he took great pleasure from their presence.

Evelyn saw him with Barbara, Louise, Hortense and Nell one
chill evening in January gambling and listening to music with much
'luxurious dallying and profaneness.'[13] If only the King had known that
this was the last time he would see all the women who had coloured his
life, warmed his bed and captured his heart. The next day Charles felt
worse for wear and asked Louise for something easy to eat, a bowl of
spoon meat – a type of soupy porridge. When his food arrived he found
he could not stomach it and instead sipped from a cup of chocolate.
He was uncomfortable throughout the night, complaining of a heaviness
in his stomach and around his heart. In the morning he still felt strange
and his servants noticed he was not his usual self. Still he tried to get
ready for the day ahead, but as he was being shaved by his barber he
collapsed, his face blackened and contorted.

The Duchess of York later recollected:

> I hastened to the chamber as soon as I was informed of his
> majesty's state. I found there, the queen, the duke of York
> (who is now king), the chancellor, and the first gentleman
> of the bed-chamber. It was a frightful spectacle, and startled
> me at first. The king was in a chair — they had placed a
> hot iron on his head, and they held his teeth open by
> force. When I had been there some time, the queen, who
> had hitherto remained speechless, came to me, and said,
> "My sister, I beseech you to tell the duke, who knows the
> king's sentiments with regard to the Catholic religion as
> well as I do, to endeavour to take advantage of some good
> moments."[14]

Charles, it appeared, wanted to convert to Catholicism – the faith of his
mother, brother and Queen – on his death bed.

Everything was done to save the King. His doctors bled, cupped,
purged and tried to save him – 'fifty-eight drugs were administered over
five days'[15] – and it seemed to be working. In joy, church bells rang out
and fires were lit across the city in celebration that evening, but then the
morning came and Charles was worse.

Bishop Ken, the man who had denied Nell lodgings, read the prayers
for the sick and dying and asked the King if he repented his sins. Charles
said he did, but when he was asked if he would take Holy Communion he
responded, 'there will be time enough yet.'[16] It seems that Louise, who
was also a Catholic, had some hand in what happened next.

She told Barillon:

> I am going to tell you the greatest secret of the world, and
> my head would be the price if they knew it! The King is a
> catholic at the bottom of his heart, but he is surrounded by
> Protestant Bishops, and no one tells him the state he is in,
> or speaks to him of God. I cannot with decency enter the
> room; besides the Queen is there nearly always. The Duke
> of York thinks of his own affairs, and he has too many to
> take that care of the King's conscience which he ought to
> do. Go and say to him, that I have conjured you to warn

him to think of what must be done to save the soul of the King. He is master in the room; he can make any one he likes go out. Lose no time, for if one delays only a little, it will be too late![17]

Louise was at least at Whitehall and could watch the toing and froing to the King's chambers, gleaning information from people as they passed by. Nell could do nothing but wait for news at home and send their son to find out what news there was of his father.

Did she know that in his heart of hearts the King wanted to die a Catholic, and did she fear whether his dying wish would be granted? In the King's sick room the Duke of York whispered to his brother, 'Sir, you have just refused the Sacrament of the Protestant Church; will you receive that of the Catholic?' and Charles replied, 'Ah, I would give everything in the world to have a priest!' The Queen's priest, Father Huddleston, was smuggled into the recess beside the King's bed. In his own words published later, the priest 'presented His Majesty with what services ... (he) could perform for God's honour and the happiness of his soul at the last hour, on which eternity depends. The King then declared that he desired to die in the faith and communion of the Holy Roman Catholic Church.'[18] James, soon to be king, stayed with his brother throughout the night.

Charles knew he didn't have much time left and begged James to look after Barbara, Duchess of Cleveland, and Louise, Duchess of Portsmouth, not to mention not allowing poor Nell to starve. He also said his goodbyes to his illegitimate sons, including Nell's. Monmouth, still in exile, was absent.

As the morning of 6 February 1685 dawned, Charles asked that the curtains be opened so that he could see the sun one last time. Content, he breathed his last at 11am. The official cause of death was apoplexy or a stroke, although rumour-mongers did their best to spread gossip that he had been poisoned.

The heralds cried out 'The King is dead – long live the King!' Nell, waiting for news, heard the bells toll and knew her King, her lover, her Charles was dead. She had not been allowed to see him to say goodbye and she was bereft beyond imagining. She could wear mourning clothes but as she was not family she was 'forbid to put her house in mourning, or to use that sort of nails about her coach and chair which it seems is kept as a distinction for the Royal Family on such occasions, and had else been put on by her command.'[19]

There was no grand funeral, no great procession and no well-attended send-off for the Restoration King. Charles had died a Catholic – although this was not well known – and a Protestant service was no longer an option. Neither was a service conducted by Catholic priests. In the end, Charles was buried at midnight on 14 of February in Westminster Abbey. Prince George of Denmark was chief mourner accompanied by the Privy Council and a few members of the royal household. Some say Nell watched the service from the back of the abbey, hiding in the shadows, to say goodbye to the man who had been her whole world.

James was proclaimed King, and, true to his promise, he would look after Charles' mistresses. Nell received a pension of £1,500 per year, the Duchess of Richmond £2,000 and the Duchess of Portsmouth £3,000. For Nell, Barbara and Frances, England was their home, but for Louise it was just a matter of time before she returned to France. Nell would finally be rid of her, though not in the way she would have liked.

Nell closed in on herself, rarely going out. She could not even bring herself to visit her beloved theatre – a place from where she rose to be by the King's side. Her whole life had been his and everything around her reminded her of him.

Chapter Nine

The Final Years 1685-1687

Charles' brother succeeded to the throne in February 1685. James II wasn't a popular choice, but as Monmouth had never been legitimised, he was the rightful heir. John Aubrey, the diarist watched the procession and ceremony and wrote:

> after the king was crowned, according to ancient custom, the peers went to the throne to kiss him. The crown was nearly kissed off his head. An earl set it right, but as the King left the Abbey for Westminster Hall, the crown tottered extremely. Just as the King came into Westminster Hall, the canopy of golden cloth carried over his head by the wardens of the Cinq Ports was torn by a puff of wind (it was a windy day). I saw the cloth hang down very lamentably. Perhaps this is an ill omen. Storm clouds of religious strife are gathering.[1]

It would indeed be an ill omen as James' reign would bring religious strife and end in his deposition.

Nell didn't attend his coronation. She didn't go anywhere. Her life had been destroyed and she kept to herself, devastated by her loss. Grief aged her and the people who were once kind began to talk of her as old and ugly. One satire even referred to her as haggard and another suggested that 'folks complain that her breath stinks of onion.'[2] Nell was now thirty-five by her 1650 birth date, or forty-three if she was born in 1642, which is more likely. At either age she was not old, just worn down and uncertain about her future.

And there were changes afoot. Although James always had a soft spot for Nell, it was not so with the other mistresses. Whereas they had all benefited financially from their relationship with Charles, the new King would not be as easy to win over. James would keep a tight rein on his purse strings. He particularly disliked Louise and had never trusted her allegiance to France. Her son lost his position as Master of the Horse, which the new King gave to his friend, the Earl of Dartmouth. It was time for Charles' French mistress to pack her bags and return to France.

Nell, never wealthy and now in fear of debtors' prison, needed James as an ally. She asked him for an audience, 'Had I suferd for my God as I have done for yr brother and you, I should not have needed other of yr kindness or justice to me. I beseech you not to doe anything to the settling of my buisness till I speake with you and apoynt me by Mr Grahams whn I may speake with you privetly. God make you as happy as my soule prayes you to be.'[3]

The Mr Grahams she referred to was in fact Colonel Richard Graham who managed the Secret Service Funds. He duly got in touch with her own secretary to find out exactly how much debt Nell was in. James granted her an audience in May and gave her £500 for the time being. She was extremely grateful, writing:

> This world is not capable of giving me a greater joy and happynes than yr Majesties favour, not as you are King and soe have it in yr poer to do me good, haveing never loved yr brother and yr selfe upon that account, but as to yr persons. Had hee lived, hee told me before he dyed, that the world shud see by what hee did for me that hee had both love and value for me ... He was my friend and allowed me to tell him all my grifes, and did not like a friend advise me and tould me who was my friend and who was not.[4]

Her debts, amounting to nearly £800, were settled and later in the year James forwarded her another £500. Her trusted acquaintance Laurence Hyde was now the Earl of Rochester after being granted her old friend's title. He tried to help out by attempting to collect revenue owing to her from 1677 on the custom on logwood, revenue that she doesn't appear to have received.

James was not a popular King. He had converted to Catholicism during his brother's reign and sought to restore the old faith to a Protestant country with religious reform. He believed in absolute monarchy and would only allow Parliament to meet once in his reign. At a time when

England was at peace, he increased his army to around 20,000 men and began to commission Catholic officers, contrary to Charles II's Test Act. Pompous, self-righteous and 'dismal' as Nell called him, it was only a matter of time before there was a rebellion, but it came from someone far closer to home than he had expected.

In June the Duke of Monmouth returned from Holland to lead a rebellion to take the crown for himself. He had always fought for his legitimacy, professing that his mother had really been married to his father, and believed himself to be the rightful heir. Lord Mulgrave, writing in his memoirs, told how Monmouth and his uncle had once been friends but 'yet a little inconstancy in one of their Mistresses (Mall Kirke), tho' in favour of a third person, was the accidental cause of the division between them, as never ceas'd till it cost one of them the hazard of his Crown, and the other that of his life on a Scaffold.'[5] Nell definitely thought Mary Kirke had shared her favours widely. When the woman had the temerity to call her a whore, Nell retorted she could take that from anyone but coming 'from an old notorious whore even before whoreing was in fashion'[6] was a step too far.

Landing at Lyme Regis, Monmouth arrived with his men and made his way to Bristol, recruiting others to his cause along the way. Their motto was 'Fear nothing but God'. The King sent his army after them. It was the first rebellion of his reign and it could not be allowed to continue. But the duke managed to get himself crowned at Taunton and, proclaiming himself to be the rightful king, continued on his way to London. The King's men clashed with Monmouth's at Sedgemoor, near Bridgwater in Somerset, on 6 July 1685 and won.

Five hundred rebels were captured but Monmouth slipped their grasp and made for the coast, intent on escape. The Royal Navy had found and taken command of his ships so he headed instead for Hampshire. The King's officers followed after him and at Ringwood he was captured after being found hiding in a ditch. Monmouth wrote to the dowager Queen Catherine from there on 9 July:

> Being in this unfortunate condition, and having non left but your majesty, that I think may have some compasion of me; and that, for the last king's sake, makes me take this boldnes to beg of you to interted for me. I would not desire your majestie to doe it, if I wear not, from the botom of my

hart, convinced how I have bine disceaved into it, and how angry God Almighty is with me for it; but I hope, madam, your intersesian will give me life to repent of it, and to show the king (James II.) how reuly and truly I will serve him hearafter; and I hope, madam, your majesty will be convinced that the life you save will ever be devoted to your service, for I have been, and ever shall be, your majesty's most dutiful and obedient servant.[7]

Nell is also thought to have asked James to spare Monmouth's life, but it was to no avail. Charles' eldest son was executed for treason on 15 July at Tower Hill. It was a brutal, bloody and bungled execution. Five blows of the axe failed to sever his head and a butcher's knife was used to finish the job.

Over 1,000 men who had followed him would be tried at the 'Bloody Assizes' that started in Winchester. On 26 August, even an old lady, Dame Alice Lyle, was sentenced to be burnt, but was then beheaded. The trials progressed throughout the West Country with over 300 people being executed and a further 800 sentenced to be transported to the West Indies. James' reign had now taken a bloody and disastrous turn.

Nell was horrified at the news. The world had changed irreparably for her. Her wonderful life with Charles was slipping into the past, becoming a cherished memory and she was struggling. She was granted a new yearly pension of £1,500 but her money only came through her trustees. She sold some of her jewellery to make ends meet, including the pearl necklace that she had bought from Peg Hughes. Nell cheered herself up by going back to the theatre, but even there it was not the same without Charles, and even less so when one Sir John Germaine decided to try his luck. She told him she 'would not lay with the dog where the deer had lain.'[8] She knew, in fact, he was having an affair with Mary Howard, the Duchess of Norfolk. She had stayed with her at Windsor and Nell had seen them slope off for a licentious night. In the morning Nell had asked the duchess where Germaine was, to which Mary replied that she didn't know. Nell responded, 'Well, we will see him come out bye and bye like a drowned rat.'[9]

Life was to get much harder for Nell when, in March 1687, she had a stroke and became partly paralysed. She was attended by one of Charles' physicians, Dr Richard Lower, and some trusted nurses. Rumours spread that she was dying but she would hold on for a while yet.

Her illness came just after an audience with James who told her that her son 'must be of the religion his father died in if she expected that he should take any care of him, and that ... the Duke's governor or tutor, a French Protestant who has been long in England, must be removed because he was a heretic and he would place another, and has placed ... a very fierce, active, discursive Papist who Harry Killigrew told the King would syllogize the Duke to death.'[10] James paid her mortgage on Bestwood Lodge later in 1687, not only that but he gave her the freehold of the estate. He was doing what he could for her but it came at a price, one she was not willing to pay, and that audience would be the last time she saw James.

The playwright Dryden had converted to Catholicism and Evelyn, after seeing Nell attend Mass with him, suspected that she was also a Catholic. It would not have been dangerous for Nell to admit it now that James was on the throne, but she had been loved as the Protestant whore and it would have been extremely damaging to her reputation. Even as she aged she was a source for gossip-mongers and there is no evidence she ever changed her faith.

Her old friend Buckingham had retired from court with James' accession. Nell had not seen him since his retirement to his manor at Helmsley in Yorkshire. In April he had been out hunting when he caught a chill. Instead of returning home, he stayed at a farmhouse rented by one of his tenants. He was feverish but felt that he would be well in a day or two. His cousin the Earl of Arran arrived to see him and sent for a doctor who confirmed that Buckingham was dying. Arran tried to convince him to talk to a priest but he didn't want one. Finally he agreed to see the local parson who asked him what his religion was. Buckingham replied, 'It is an insignificant question. I have been a shame and disgrace to all religions – but if you can do me any good, do.'[11] He died on 16 April 1687 without making a will. In his pocket was a notebook with his ideas for poems and plays. He had also written: 'To what situation am I now reduced! Is this odious little hut a suitable lodging for a prince? ... I am afflicted with poverty and haunted by remorse; despised by my country, and I fear forsaken by my God. I am forsaken by all my acquaintances, neglected by the friends of my bosom.'[12]

He was buried with great pomp and ceremony on 7 June 1687 in Henry VII's chapel in Westminster Abbey, but Nell was too ill to go. She had not forgotten him nor forsaken him. In June she was told she was dying and her first thoughts turned to her son Charles who was fighting abroad.

One biographer suggested that she could not stay at her house in Pall Mall because the roof was leaking so she moved four doors down to her friend Hannah Grace's. There is no other mention of this lady, nor that Nell was not at home when she became bedridden. By most accounts Nell had a second stroke in May and was at home in her beautiful silver bed. 'Mrs Nelly has bine dying of an apoplexie. She is now come to her sense on one side, for ye other is dead of a palsey. She is thought to be worth 100,000li; 2000li in revenue and ye rest in jewels and plate.'[13]

She wrote her will, leaving everything to her son. She appointed four executors – her friend Laurence Hyde, Henry Sidney, Thomas Herbert, the 8th Earl of Pembroke and Sir Robert Sawyer, James' attorney-general – to ensure her wishes were carried out. It began:

> I, Ellen Gwynne, of the parish of St. Martin-in-the-fields, and county of Middlesex, spinster, this 9th day of July, anno Domini 1687, do make this my last will and testament, and do revoke all former wills. First, in hope of a joyful resurrection, I do recommend myself whence I came, my soul into the hands of Almighty God, and my body unto the earth, to be decently buried, at the discretion of my executors, hereinafter named; and as for all such houses, lands, tenements, offices, places, pensions, annuities, and hereditaments whatsoever, in England, Ireland, or elsewhere, wherein I, or my heirs, or any to the use of, or in trust for me or my heirs, hath, have, or may or ought to have, any estate, right, claim or demand whatsoever, of fee-simple or freehold, I give and devise the same all and wholly to my dear natural son, his Grace the Duke of St. Alban' s, and to the heirs of his body; and as for all and all manner of my jewels, plate, household stuff, goods, chattels, credits, and other estate whatsoever, I give and bequeath the same.[14]

In July she had a new doctor in Christian Harell, another of the King's physicians, who would charge £109 for his care and remedies. James also sent two of his own doctors, Dr Le Febre and Dr Lister, but all they could really do was relieve her physical pain and give her some comfort in her final days. She had another regular visitor in Dr Tenison, the vicar of St Martin-in-the-Fields, who sat by her bedside and listened to her reminiscence on days gone past. He provided solace and support when Nell knew her time was short.

On 18 October 1687 she added a codicil to her will for her son to carry out.

1. That I may be buried in the Church of St Martin-in-the-Fields;
2. That Dr Tenison may preach my funeral sermon;
3. That there may be a decent pulpit cloth and cushion given to St Martin-in-the-Fields;
4. That (the Duke of St Albans) would give one hundred pounds for the use of the poor of the said St Martin-in-the-Fields and St James Westminster, to be given into the hands of the said Dr Tenison for taking any poor debtors of the said parish out of prison, and cloaths this winter, and other necessaries as he shall find most fit;
5. That for showing my charity to those who differ from me in religion, I desire that fifty pounds may be put into the hands of Dr Tenison and Mr Warner, who, taking to them any two persons of the Roman religion, may dispose of it for the use of the poor of that religion inhabiting the parish of St James aforesaid;
6. That Mrs Rose Forster may have two hundred pounds given to her, any time within a year after my decease;
7. That Jo my porter may have ten pounds given to him;
8. That my present nurses may have ten pounds and mourning, besides the wages due to each;
9. That my present servants may have mourning each, and a year's wages, beside their wages due;
10. That the Lady Fairborne may have fifty pounds given to her to buy a ring;
11. That my kinsman, Mr Cholmley, may have one hundred pounds given to him, within a year after this date;
12. That His Grace would please to lay out twenty pounds yearly for the releasing of poor debtors out of prison every Christmas Day;
13. That Mr John Warner may have fifty pounds given him to buy a ring;
14. That the Lady Hollyman may have the pension of ten shillings per week continued to her during the said lady's life.[15]

*****

Nell died around 10pm on 14 November 1687 of heart failure, although rumours still talked of syphilis, 'a parting gift from the King' the most vicious whispered. She was buried on the seventeenth. Her send-off was attended by hundreds of people who filled the church and lined the streets. She had asked to be buried in a plain black coffin, but given the cost of her funeral, it must have been extravagant. The funeral expenses were £375, paid by Sir Stephen Fox, in lieu of her pension from James.

Dr Tenison gave the sermon, although Nell had been worried it would stop his advancement. It certainly caused a stir, but his relationship with Nell in her last days was important to him. Some say Tenison gave her his space in the vicar's vault, others that she was placed next to her mother. The real location of her burial is lost.

In 1691, when Tenison was under consideration for a bishopric in Lincoln, it was suggested that it would be improper because of his association with Nell. Queen Mary later said, 'If I can read a man's heart through his looks, had she not made a truly pious end the Doctor could never have been induced to speak well of her.'[16] He would later become Archbishop of Canterbury. We don't know what he preached in his sermon but *An Elegy in Commemoration of Madam Eleanor Gwyn* ran thus:

> some may cast objections in and say
> These scattered praises that we seek to lay
> Upon her hearse are but the formal way.
> Yet when we tell them she was free from strife,
> Courteous even to the poor, no pride of life,
> E'er entertaining, but did much abound
> In charity, and for it was renowned;
> Not seeking praises, but did vain praise despise,
> And at her alms were heard no trumpet noise;
> And how again we let them further see
> That she refused and hated flattery,
> And far from her dessemblers did command,
> We may have hopes her fame for this will stand[17]

The codicil or addition to Nell's will was not proven until 19 July 1688. The first will had been approved by Nell's son, the Duke of St Albans, and proved in common form at the prerogative court, but he was unaware of his mother's additions. John Warner, Nell's chaplain and the writer of the codicil, presented it at the next court hearing, but witnesses, including her housemaid, Elizabeth Leverett, her friend Anne Edline, and her doctors, Le Febre and Harrell, were called to attest to its authenticity. Warner also mentioned other requests that had not been added but that were Nell's wishes – Mrs Jennings was to have a mourning ring, Orange Nan to have five pounds and Warner himself to have her silver tea table and pots, but these last items were not proved. Warner may have been remembering other people Nell wanted to look out for but he may also have been chancing his arm.

Many of the men who had surrounded Nell and the King – his Merry Gang – had died. Gone were Buckingham, Rochester, Jermyn, Savile and Scrope. Nell had seen her friends pass away over the past few years and must have felt their loss even though she felt the King's passing more deeply than any. Life was never the same without him and out of all his mistresses she was the one who mourned him the most. She was also the first of Charles' mistresses to succumb to a fatal illness.

Hortense Mancini had managed to live relatively well after the King's death. Her lover, Charles de Saint-Évremond, the prolific essayist and literary critic, who was nearly forty years her senior, lived with her in Paradise Row, Chelsea. He once described 'the movements of her mouth have charm, and the queerest grimaces become her wonderfully when she is imitating those who make them. Her smile would soften the hardest heart and lighten the profoundest dejection of mind.'[18] She was still welcomed at court by her niece, Mary of Modena, but she had taken to drinking heavily, especially gin, whisky and absinthe.

Evelyn wrote, 'She has written her own story and adventures, and so has her other extravagant sister, wife to the noble family of Colonna.'[19] Hortense and one of her sisters, Marie Mancini, were some of the first women in France to print their memoirs. In them, they related their relationships with their estranged husbands. Hortense's still wanted her back and, in her last years, constantly asked her to return to France. When this didn't work, he took a legal case against her to try to force her return which he believed was in her best interest 'as the greatest proof I could give her of an enduring affection for her, so that she can be cured of a sort of spiritual gangrene of which she herself is not conscious.'[20] She was ordered to return to France and stay in a convent for six months before returning to her husband, but she was never going to do that.

She died on 9 November 1699 at home. Evelyn wrote that she had 'hastened her death by intemperate drinking strong spirits,'[21] but others suggested she may have taken her own life. Strangely, her husband seized her coffin and took her body with him in a macabre procession around his estates in France before she was finally interred next to the tomb of her uncle, Cardinal Mazarin in the College des Quatre-Nations in Paris.

Frances Stuart, immortalised as Britannia on British coins, had a happy marriage with the man with whom she eloped, the Duke of Richmond. When her husband became the English ambassador in Denmark, she managed their business affairs and estates, no longer the empty-headed girl who had built castles from playing cards. After his death, these estates reverted back to the Crown as they had had no children and there were no heirs. She kept Cobham Hall in Kent, but would later get caught up in legal wrangles over its ownership. However, she did manage to amass a small fortune through her own properties. She often attended court and made her last public appearance at the coronation of Queen Anne in April 1702. Frances died a few months later and was buried close to her husband in the Richmond family vault in Westminster Abbey.

Queen Catherine returned to Portugal in 1692. Catherine was happy enough to live a quiet and simple life in her final years at her palace at Bemposta in Lisbon, but her brother Pedro, King of Portugal, named her as regent in 1705. This once quiet and timid Queen, who had put up with all of the King's mistresses and kept to the background, now came into power. She saw her country through the war of succession and directed Portugal's campaign against the French with decisiveness and precision, proving herself to be an effective, just and triumphant ruler.

No one expected her sudden death the same year when she was suddenly gripped with acute stomach pains. By 10pm on 31 December she was dead at the age of sixty-seven. Crowds gathered for her final journey from Bemposta Palace to Belem monastery where she was interred. Lisbon closed down for eight days and for a year afterwards the court stayed in mourning for Charles II's Queen and Portugal's Queen Regent.

Barbara had returned to England in 1682 after spending some time in France. She had not married and continued to have affairs with several men, including the actor Cardell Goodman. Her sons were unhappy with the match and had him arrested for highway robbery. He was imprisoned in Newgate in the summer of 1684 but released by autumn. Not happy that their mother's lover had his freedom, they had him charged with employing Alexander Amadei to poison two of them, the Duke of Grafton and the Duke of Northumberland. He was found guilty and fined £1,000 but in 1685 Barbara persuaded James II to pardon him.

After this scandal ended Barbara felt the need to settle down and was completely enamoured with Major-General Beau Fielding, marrying him on 25 November 1705. Unlucky in love, she didn't know he was already married and that she had been duped. Fielding was just after her money and had recently married Mary Wadsworth thinking she was a wealthy widow named Mrs Deleau. The marriage was a pure deception. Mrs Deleau's servants had suspected Fielding was a conman and her hairdresser, Charlotte Villars, disguised Mary Wadsworth, one of her friends, as the widow. Fielding didn't have a clue who he was really marrying just weeks before Barbara.

Barbara was unaware for some time that her marriage was bigamous but she soon realised that her new husband was having an affair with her granddaughter, Charlotte Calvert, who was living with her after her own failed marriage. In June 1706 Mary Wadsworth visited Barbara and told her the story. When she confronted Fielding, he attacked her and Barbara had to scream for help from a window. He was arrested and subsequently charged with adultery. The marriage was annulled in May 1707. Barbara lived in what is now known as Walpole House in Chiswick until her death of dropsy or heart failure which had 'swelled her gradually to a monstrous bulk'[22] in October 1709. She was buried in the cemetery there.

Nell would have turned in her grave if she had known that, out of them all, Louise lived the longest. She had returned to France in the autumn of 1685, fully aware that she was not popular in England and could no longer call it her home.

But in France she had her enemies, too and in 1686 her gossip and disrespect of King Louis XIV's mistress, Madame de Maintenon, was reported to the King. He had an official letter drawn up banning her from court, but the old French ambassador and supporter of Louise, Courtin, saw it and intervened on her behalf. The King allowed her an audience where she protested her innocence, but she was told in no uncertain terms to curb her mouth or face further displeasure.

Louise faced financial difficulties with the accession of William III who stopped her pension and it was Louis who continued to pay her £12,000 a year for her services to France. When later there were several lawsuits from creditors seeking payment, the French king intervened on her behalf but she would still be forced to sell off some of her possessions to cover her expenses.

She occasionally visited England to see her family. Her son had returned from France to live there and on 8 January 1692 he married Anne Brudenell. They had three children, Charles, Louisa and Anne. Louise wrote to them frequently but she became a lonely figure as she got older, staying mostly to herself on her estates at Aubigny. She never married and instead turned her attention to the plight of the local people – something she had never done in England.

In 1692 she wrote to the Controller-General of France: 'The extreme misery of the people and peasants in the country surrounding Aubigny, which is my Duchy, makes me, Monsieur, plead urgently with you to have pity on the unhappy condition to which they are reduced.'[23]

She was back in England for the coronation of George I in 1714. At the celebrations the Countess of Dorchester remarked, 'Who would have thought we three whores should have met here?' when she met up with Louise and the Countess of Orkney. They had all been mistresses for successive kings over a period of twenty years. Louise, who would never call herself a whore, would have been mortified.

She died on 14 November 1734, on a trip to Paris to consult with physicians. Her health had been poor over the past few years yet she had reached the ripe old age of eighty-five and outlived all the other mistresses.

*****

Whereas Charles II's lovers would be remembered for their passions, scandals and intrigues, Nell was the steadfast one. Colley Cibber wrote of her: 'If the common fame of her may be believed, which in my memory was not doubted, she had less to be laid to her charge than any other of those ladies who were in the same state of preferment. She never meddled in matters of any serious moment, or was the tool of working politicians. Never broke into those amorous infidelities which others are accused of; but was as visibly distinguished by her particular personal inclination for the king as her rivals were by their titles and grandeur.'[24]

The orange girl who captured the hearts of the nation would pass into memory as pretty, witty Nell, the actress who stole a king's heart and loved him unconditionally.

Epilogue

Nell outshone all of Charles II's other mistresses as the one who would stay in the nation's memory. There is just something so intriguing about a rags to riches story that calls to us all. She was a Restoration-age Cinderella who never forgot where she came from, or the people who supported her, and she has been immortalised in many ways.

In London she is remembered with a statue, complete with a King Charles cavalier spaniel at her feet, standing prominently above the entrance to Nell Gwynn House, in Sloane Avenue. The ten-storey block of art-deco style flats was built in 1937. It is the only statue of a royal mistress in London. There is also a fountain of Venus in Sloane Square and on the urn at the base sit Charles and Nell, together for eternity.

There have been stories that her health is drunk at the Royal Hospital Chelsea. A pageant held there in 1908 by the Chelsea Pageant's Historical Committee saw ten performances depicting events that 'appeared to them to cover and focus, as far as possible, the history of Chelsea, and to introduce the largest number of those historical characters which are identified with the locality.' Nell was one of those historical characters who appeared alongside Charles II, played by Tom Heslewood, the pageant's lead costume designer, to tell the story of the founding of the hospital.

Her home at 79 Pall Mall has a blue plaque that reads, 'In a house on this site lived Nell Gwynne from 1671–1687'. While in Hereford the council has one on the site they believe is her birthplace. It reads, 'Site of the birth of Nell Gwynne, Founder of the Chelsea Hospital and mother of the first Duke of St Albans, Born 1650, Died 1687, The House was demolished in 1858'. Lauderdale House has a pink plaque that states she briefly lived there.

Interestingly, Whitecross Street Prison also has a blue plaque that commemorates Nell's charitable nature and the donation she left in her will. It states, 'Whitecross Debtors Prison 1813–1870. Warm-hearted Nell Gwynne, in her will, desired her natural son the Duke of St. Albans, to lay out £20 a year, known as "Nell Gwynne's bounty", to release poor debtors out of prison, and this sum was distributed every Christmas Day to the inmates of Whitecross Street Prison.'

There are several pubs carrying her name, including Nell Gwynn Tavern in Covent Garden, built on the site of the Old Bull Inn. A nursery school bears her name, as do varieties of fuchsia and chrysanthemum. In 1910 Yardley produced a Nell Gwynne perfume that was 'enchanting and lasting'. She would have loved that!

A more unusual tribute to Nell, known locally as 'Nell Gwyn's Monument', is a stone obelisk in Tring Park, Hertfordshire. Local stories tell that Nell and Charles used Tring Mansion as a romantic getaway. The obelisk is 50ft (15m) tall and mothers would tell their children to run around it until an orange fell off the top.

As with many places, the link to Nell is tenuous, but it's a lovely story. Tring mansion was designed by Sir Christopher Wren and built in 1685, but though its history states it was visited several times by Charles II, it would have been impossible given he died in February of that year. Another story says their romantic getaway was Dunsley House and legend remembers it was called 'Elinors' after Nell, and a walk from the nearby mansion to Dunsley House was called 'The Nell Gwyn Avenue'.

When Lord Rothschild acquired Tring Park Estate he tried to prove that Nell had lived there, but the only connection he discovered was to Charles II and his finance minister, Henry Guy, to whom he granted the Manor of Tring. Still, local rumours do often have a basis in fact and the couple might well have visited on occasion.

Nell has been immortalised in books, plays and film over the years. She appeared as a character in a play from as early as 1799, *The Peckham Frolic: or Nell Gwyn*, a comedy in three acts by Edward Jerningham, and most recently in 2015 in *Nell Gwynne: A Dramatick Essaye on Acting and Prostitution* by Bella Merlin, and *Nell Gwynn* by Jessica Swale. An early film from 1911, based on a play of the same name, *Sweet Nell of Old Drury*, brings the actress to life, as does the 1934 film *Nell Gwynn*, starring Anna Neagle. A more modern take on Charles, Nell and other characters of the Restoration can be found in the 2003 series *Charles II: The Power and The Passion*. And if you're looking for more on Rochester,

The Libertine with Johnny Depp is immensely watchable, though, as in many film adaptations of Nell's life, not entirely historically accurate.

But out of all the ways in which Nell has been remembered my favourite, and I think probably hers too, would be on 1950s advertising for Crosbie's Nell Gwyn marmalade. This one would have made her laugh out loud!

Appendix I

Charles Beauclerk, Duke of St Albans

Nell's son Charles had his father's looks. He was seventeen when his mother died, in effect leaving him orphaned. Not long after her death, he left for Hungary with his tutor. When back in England he continued to live at their family home at Pall Mall. He had an income from his position as Grand Falconer of England, in charge of ten falconers and over twenty feeders, and was paid around £1,370 a year, although he had to cover the costs of his job. He was responsible for providing the King, now his uncle, with hawks on his hunting trips and making sure they were well looked after.

Nell left everything to her son, but it included debts of £6,900 she owed to Childs Bank. Some of her silver was sold to pay off part of the debt and St Albans would pay the rest, but he also had to borrow £8,000 from Lord Clare, one of the bank's richest customers in the 1690s. In 1686 he let Burford House to James' son-in-law, Prince George of Denmark, for £260 a year. He had some income from his mother's pension and one of £2,000 a year from Queen Catherine that would be paid up until her death.

In 1687 he was appointed Colonel of the Princess of Denmark's Regiment of Horse, but he had yet to gain any military experience so Colonel Langston was left in charge while he fought for the Holy Roman Emperor Leopold I under Prince Charles of Lorraine. He distinguished himself at the Battle of Belgrade, a bloody foray against the Turks, and he returned home with two Turkish boys who had been taken prisoner.

Both his uncle and his father's wife, Queen Catherine, tried to persuade him to convert to Catholicism but he resisted and would come to support William of Orange's campaign against the old faith. James was deposed in 1688 in the 'Glorious Revolution' and St Albans would become a favourite of the new King, William III, who described him as 'of a black complexion not so tall as the Duke of Northumberland, yet very like King Charles.'

His regiment was disbanded after their defeat at the battle of Steinkirk in 1692, but the following year he fought under William of Orange at the Battle of Neerwinden and was later made Captain of the Band of Gentlemen Pensioners, who were William's personal escort. He was so close to the King that his friends nicknamed him 'Prince Orange'.

After his marriage in 1694 to Lady Diana de Vere, daughter of Aubrey de Vere, 20th Earl of Oxford, he spent more time at home, which was now Burford House. The couple would go on to have twelve children, from which the current Duke of St Albans is descended, with the title passing through the male heir's bloodline. Charles and Diana would have nine sons – Charles, William, Vere, Henry, Sidney, George, Seymour, James and Aubrey – and three daughters – Diana, Mary and Anne.

In 1694 he became a Lord of the Bedchamber with a salary of £1,000 a year and a further pension of £2,000 per annum. He was given the position of Ambassador Extraordinary to France from December 1697 to January 1698 and visited Versailles to meet Louis XIV. But for all his positions he was still often in debt.

When Queen Anne came to power, his roles at court diminished, but his wife became First Lady of the Bedchamber. After Anne's death in 1707, George I took the throne and St Albans was restored to his position as Captain of the Gentlemen Pensioners and his wife became Mistress of the Robes and Lady of the Stole. Other positions followed as Lord Lieutenant of Berkshire and High Steward of Windsor, culminating in his receiving the Garter in 1718.

St Albans had a long and colourful career and a large family to look after him in his dotage. He died on 10 May 1726 in Bath after a long illness and was buried in Westminster Abbey.

Appendix II

A Panegyric Upon Nelly

Once attributed to John Wilmot, Earl of Rochester, 1681.

Of a great heroine I mean to tell,
And by what just degrees her titles swell
To Mrs Nelly grown, from cinder Nell.
Much did she suffer first on bulk and stage
From the blackguard and bullies of the age;
Much more her growing virtue did sustain,
While dear Charles Hart and Buckhurst sued in vain.
In vain they sued; cursed be the envious tongue
That her undoubted chastity would wrong,
For should we fame believe, we then might say
That thousands lay with her, as well as they.
But, fame, thou liest, for her prophetic mind
Foresaw her greatness. Fate had well designed.
And her ambition chose to be before
A virtuous countess, an imperial whore.
Even in her native dirt her soul was high
And did at crowns and shining monarchs fly;
E'en while she cinders raked, her swelling breast
With thoughts of glorious whoredom was possessed;
Still did she dream (nor did her birth withstand)
Of dangling sceptres in her dirty hand.
But first the basket her fair arm did suit,
Laden with pippins and Hesperian fruit,
This first step raised, to th'wandering pit she sold
The lovely fruit, smiling with streaks of gold.
Fate now for her did its whole force engage,
And from the pit she's mounted to the stage;

There in full lustre did her glories shine,
And, long eclipsed, spread forth their light divine;
There Hart's and Rowley's soul she did ensnare,
And made a king the rival to a player.
The king o'ercomes; and to the royal bed
The dunghill-offspring is in triumph led –
Nor let the envious her first rags object
To her, that's now in tawdry gayness decked.
Her merit does from this much greater show,
Mounting so high, that took her rise so low.
Less famed that Nelly was whose cuckold rage
In ten years wars did half the world engage.
She's now the darling strumpet of the crowd,
Forgets her state, and talks to them aloud;
Lays by her greatness, and descends to prate
With those 'bove whom she's raised by wond'rous fate;
True to th'Protestant government and laws;
The choice delight of the whole mobile,
Scarce Monmouth's self is more belov'd than she.
Was this the cause that did their quarrel move,
That both are rivals to the people's love?
No, twas her matchless loyalty alone
That bids prince Perkin pack up and be gone.
Illbred thou art, says prince. Nell does reply,
Was Mrs Barlow better bred than I?
Thus sneak'd away the nephew overcome;
By aunt-in-law's severer wit struck dumb.
Her virtue, loyalty, wit and noble mind
In the foregoing doggerel you may find.
Now, for her piety, one touch, and then
To Rymer I'll resign my muse and pen.
Twas thus that raised her charity so high,
To visit those that did in durance lie;
From Oxford prisons many did she free –
There died her father, and there gloried she
In giving others life and liberty.
So pious a remembrance still she bore
E'en to the fetters that her father wore.

Nor was her mother's funeral less her care,
No cost, no velvet did the daughter spare:
Fine gilded 'scutchions did the hearse enrich,
To celebrate the martyr of the ditch.
Burnt brandy did in flaming brimmers flow,
Drunk at her funeral; while her well-pleased shade
Rejoiced, e'en in the sober fields below,
At all the drunkenness her death had made.

Was ever child with such a mother blessed?
Or even mother such a child possessed?
Nor must her cousin be forgot, preferred
From many years command in the black-guard
To be a ensign;-
Whose tattered colours well do represent
His first estate i'th'ragged regiment.
Thus we in short have all the virtues seen
Of the incomparable madam Gwyn;
Nor wonder, others are not with her shown;
She who no equal has, must be alone.

Appendix III

Meet Alexander Bendo

Nell helped Rochester promote his alter ego with this flyer:

TO ALL
Gentlemen, Ladies, and others,
Whether of
CITY, TOWN, or COUNTRY:
ALEXANDER BENDO
Wisheth all Health and Prosperity.

Whereas this famed metropolis of England (and were the endeavours of its worthy inhabitants equal to their power, merit, and virtue, I should not stick to denounce it, in a short time, the metropolis of the whole world); whereas, I say, this city (as most great ones are) has ever been infested with a numerous company of such whose arrogant confidence, backing their ignorance, has enabled them to impose on the people either premeditated cheats, or at best the palpable dull and empty mistakes of their self-deluded imagination, in physic, chymical and Galenic; in astrology, physiognomy, palmistry, mathematics, alchimy, and even in government itself; the last of which I will not propose to discourse of, or meddle at all in, since it in no way belongs to my trade or vocation, as the rest do; which (thanks to my God) I find much more safe, I think equally honest, and therefore more profitable.

But as to all the former, they have been so erroneously practis'd by many unlearned wretches, whom poverty and neediness for the most part (if not the restless itch of deceiving) has forc'd to straggle and wander in unknown parts, that even the professions themselves, though originally the products of the most learned and wise men's laborious studies and experience, and by them left a wealthy and glorious inheritance for ages to come, seem by this bastard race of quacks and cheats to have been run out of all wisdom, learning, perspicuousness, and truth, with which they were so plentifully stocked; and now run into a repute of mere mists, imaginations, errors, and deceits, such as in the management of these idle professors indeed they were.

You will therefore (I hope) gentlemen, ladies, and others, deem it but just, that I who for some years have with all faithfulness and assiduity courted these arts, and received such signal favours from them, that they have admitted me to the happy and full enjoyment of themselves, and trusted me with their greatest secrets, should with an earnestness and concern more than ordinary, take their parts against those impudent fops, whose saucy, impertinent addresses and pretensions have brought such a scandal upon their most immaculate honours and reputations.

Besides, I hope you will not think I could be so imprudent, that if I had intended any such foul play myself, I would have given you so fair warning by my severe observations upon others, *Qui alterum incusant probri, ipsum se intueri oportet*, Plaut. However, gentlemen, in a world like this, (where virtue is so exactly counterfeited, and hypocrisy so generally taken notice of, that every one, armed with suspicion, stands upon his guard against it) 'twill be very hard for a stranger especially to escape censure. All I shall say for myself on this score is this, if I appear to any one like a counterfeit, even for the sake of that chiefly ought I to be construed a true man, who is the counterfeit's example, his original, and that which he employs his industry and pains to imitate and copy. Is it therefore my fault if the cheat by his wits and endeavours makes himself so like me, that consequently I cannot avoid resembling of him? Consider, pray, the valiant and the coward, the wealthy merchant and the bankrupt, the politician and the fool; they are the same in many things, and differ in but one alone. The valiant man holds up his head, looks confidently round about him, wears a sword, courts a lord's wife, and owns it; so does the coward: one only point of honour, and that's courage (which like false metal, one only trial can discover) makes the distinction.

The bankrupt walks the exchange, buys, bargains, draws bills, and accepts them with the richest, whilst paper and credit are current coin: that which makes the difference is real cash; a great defect indeed, and yet but one, and that the last found out, and still till then the least perceived.

Now for the politician, he is a grave, deliberating, close, prying man: Pray are there not grave, deliberating, close, prying fools? If then the difference betwixt all these (though infinite in effect) be so nice in all appearance, will you expect it should be otherwise betwixt the false physician, astrologer, &c., and the true? The first calls himself learned doctor, sends forth his bills, gives physic and counsel, tells and foretells; the other is bound to do just as much: 'tis only your experience must distinguish betwixt them, to which I willingly submit myself: I'll only say something to the honour of the Mountebank, in case you discover me to be one.

Reflect a little what kind of creature 'tis, he is one then who is fain to supply some higher ability he pretends to, with craft, he draws great companies to him by undertaking strange things which can never be effected. The politician (by his example no doubt) finding how the people are taken with specious, miraculous, impossibilities, plays the same game; protests, declares, promises I know not what things, which he's sure can ne'er be brought about. The people believe, are deluded and pleased; the expectation of a future good which shall never befall them draws their eyes off a present evil. Thus are they kept and establish'd in subjection, peace, and obedience; he in greatness, wealth, and power. So you see the politician is, and must be a mountebank in state affairs; and the mountebank no doubt, if he thrives, is an errant politician in physic.

But that I may not prove too tedious, I will proceed faithfully to inform you, what are the things in which I pretend chiefly at this time to serve my country.

First, I will (by the leave of God) perfectly cure that *Labes Britannica*, or grand English disease, the scurvy; and that with such ease to my patient, that he shall not be sensible of the least inconvenience whilst I steal his distemper from him; I know there are many, who treat this disease with mercury, antimony, spirits, and salts, being dangerous remedies, in which I shall meddle very little, and with great caution, but by more secure, gentle, and less fallible medicines, together with the observation of some few rules in diet, perfectly cure the patient, having freed him from all the symptoms, as looseness of the teeth, scorbutick spots, want of appetite, pains and lassitude in the limbs and joints, especially the legs. And to say truth, there are few distempers in this nation that are not, or at least proceed not originally from the scurvy; which were it well rooted out (as I make no question to do it from all those who shall come into my hands) there would not be heard of so many gouts, aches, dropsies, and consumptions; nay, even those thick and slimy humours which generate stones in the kidneys and bladder, are for the most part offsprings of the scurvy. It would prove tedious to set down all its malignant race; but those who address themselves here, shall be still informed by me in the nature of their distempers, and the grounds I proceed upon to their cure: so will all reasonable people be satisfied that I treat them with care, honesty, and understanding; for I am not of their opinion who endeavour to render their vocations rather mysterious, than useful and satisfactory.

I will not here make a catalogue of diseases and distempers; it behoves a physician I am sure to understand them all; but if any come to me (as I think there are very few that have escap'd my practice) I shall not be ashamed to own to my patient, where I find myself to seek, and at least he shall be secure with me from having experiments tried upon him; a privilege he can never hope to enjoy, either in the hands of the grand doctors of the court and town, or in those of the lesser quacks and mountebanks.

It is fit though that I assure you of great secrecy as well as care in diseases, where it is requisite, whether venereal or others, as some peculiar to women, the green sickness, weaknesses, inflammations, or obstructions in the stomach, reins, liver, spleen, &c. (for I would put no word in my bill that bears any unclean sound; it is enough that I make myself understood; I have seen physician's bills as bawdy as *Aretin's Dialogues*, which no man that walks warily before God can approve of) but I cure all suffocations in those parts producing fits of the mother, convulsions, nocturnal inquietudes, and other strange accidents not fit to be set down here, persuading young women very often that their hearts are like to break for love, when God knows the distemper lies far enough from that place.

Likewise barrenness (proceeding from any accidental cause, as it often falls out, and no natural defect; for nature is easily assisted, difficultly restored, but impossible to be made more perfect by Man than God himself had at first created and bestowed it). Cures of this kind I have done signal and many, for the which I doubt not but I have the good wishes and hearty prayers of many families, who had else pin'd out their days under the deplorable and reproachful misfortunes of barren wombs, leaving plentiful estates and possessions to be inherited by strangers.

As to astrological predictions, physiognomy, divination by dreams, and otherwise (palmistry I have not faith in, because there can be no reason alleged for it) my own experience has convinc'd me more of their considerable effects, and marvellous operations, chiefly in the directions of future proceedings, to the avoiding of dangers that threaten, and laying hold of advantages that might offer themselves

I say, my own practice has convinc'd me more than all the sage and wise writings extant of those matters; for I might say this for myself (did it not look like ostentation) that I have very seldom failed in my predictions, and often been very serviceable in my advice. How far I am capable in this way I am sure is not fit to be delivered in print: those who have no opinion of the truth of this art, will not I suppose come to me about it; such as have, I make no question of giving them ample satisfaction.

Nor will I be ashamed to set down here my willingness to practise rare secrets (though somewhat collateral to my profession), for the help, conservation, and augmentation of beauty and comeliness; a thing created at first by God, chiefly for the glory of his own name, and then for the better establishment of mutual love between man and woman; for when God had bestowed on man the power of strength and wisdom, and thereby rendered woman liable to the subjection of his absolute will, it seemed but requisite that she should be endued likewise in recompense, with some quality that might beget in him admiration of her, and so enforce his tenderness and love.

The knowledge of these secrets I gathered in my travels abroad (where I have spent my time ever since I was fifteen years old to this my nine and twentieth year) in France and Italy. Those that have travelled in Italy will tell you to what a miracle Art does there assist Nature in the preservation of beauty; how women of forty bear the same countenance with those of fifteen: ages are no ways there distinguished by faces; whereas here in England look a horse in the mouth, and a woman in the face, you presently know both their ages to a year. I will therefore give you such remedies, that without destroying your complexion (as most of your paints and daubings do) shall render them perfectly fair, clearing and preserving them from all spots, freckles, heats, and pimples, nay, marks of the small-pox, or any other accidental ones, so the face be not seam'd or scarr'd.

I will also cleanse and preserve your teeth white and round as pearls, fastening them that are loose: your gums shall be kept entire, and red as coral; your lips of the same colour, and soft as you could wish your lawful kisses.

I will likewise administer that which shall cure the worst breath, provided the lungs be not totally perished and imposthumated; as also certain and infallible remedies for those whose breaths are yet untainted, so that nothing but either a very long sickness or old age itself shall ever be able to spoil them.

I will, besides (if it be desired) take away from their fatness who have overmuch, and add flesh to those that want it, without the least detriment to their constitutions.

Now should Galen himself look out of his grave, and tell me these were baubles below the profession of a physician, I would boldly answer him, that I take more glory in preserving God's image, in its unblemished beauty upon one good face, than I should do in patching up all the decay'd carcasses in the world.

They that will do me the favour to come to me, shall be sure from three of the clock in the afternoon till eight at night at my lodgings in Tower-street, next door to the sign of the Black Swan, at a goldsmith's house to find

Their humble servant,
ALEXANDER BENDO.

Endnotes

Chapter One: The Early Years 1650-1662

1. Anon, *A Panegyric upon Nelly*
2. Melville, *Nell Gwyn: The Story of Her Life*, p. 29
3. Hopkins, *Nell Gwynne*, p.7
4. MacGregor-Hastie, *Nell Gwyn*, p.17
5. Thornbury, 'St Giles-in-the-Fields', in *Old and New London*, pp. 197-218. British History Online http://www.british-history.ac.uk/old-new-london/vol3/pp197-218 [accessed 11 August 2020].
6. Bevan, *Nell Gwyn*, p. 22
7. Melville, *Nell Gwyn: The Story of Her Life*, p. 30
8. *Thornbury,* 'Covent Garden: Part 1 of 3', in *Old and New London*, pp. 238-255. British History Online http://www.british-history.ac.uk/old-new-london/vol3/pp238-255 [accessed 11 August 2020].
9. Pepys, *The Diary of Samuel Pepys,* 26 October 1667
10. Parker, *Nell Gwyn*, p. 9
11. Princess Michael of Kent, *Cupid and the King*, p. 2
12. CSP, Venice
13. Ibid.
14. Pepys, *The Diary of Samuel Pepys,* 21 May 1662
15. Strickland, *Lives of the Queens of England*, Vol VIII, p. 305
16. Evelyn, *The Diary of John Evelyn,* 23 August 1662, loc. 6301
17. Strickland, *Lives of the Queens of England*, Vol VIII, p. 332
18. Ibid, Vol VIII, p. 323
19. Pepys, *The Diary of Samuel Pepys*, 7 September 1662
20. Strickland, *Lives of the Queens of England*, Vol VIII, p. 333
21. Savile, *Character of King Charles the Second*, p. 13
22. Howe, *The First English Actresses*, p. 25

23. Smith, *Foreign Visitors in England: And what They Have Thought of Us: Being Some Notes on Their Books and Their Opinions During the Last Three Centuries,* p. 211

Chapter Two: On the Stage 1663-1665

1. Betterton, *The History of the English Stage from the Restauration to the Present Time*, p. 111
2. MacGregor-Hastie, *Nell Gwyn*, p.32
3. Wilson, *The Court Wits of the Restoration*, p.37
4. Beauclerk, *Nell Gwyn*, p. 40
5. Wilson, *Court Satires of the Restoration*, p.100
6. Cunningham, *London: Being a Comprehensive Survey of the History, Tradition & Historical Associations of Buildings & Monuments, Arranged Under Streets in Alphabetical Order*, p.433
7. Arnold, *City of Sin: London and its Vices*, p.88
8. Chesterton, *Nell Gwyn*, p. 29
9. McEnery, *Corpus Linguistics and 17th Century Prostitution*, p. 52
10. Zuvich, *Sex and Sexuality in Stuart Britain*, p. 41
11. Fisk, *The Cambridge Companion to English Restoration Theatre*, p. 1
12. Pepys, *The Diary of Samuel Pepys*, 24 May 1660
13. Ibid, 13 February 1667-1668
14. Ibid, 8 May 1663
15. Beauclerk, *Nell Gwyn*, p. 57
16. Anon, *A Panegyric on Nelly*
17. Pepys, *The Diary of Samuel Pepys*, 9 March 1668-1669
18. McEnery, *Corpus Linguistics and 17th Century Prostitution*, p. 288
19. Ibid.
20. Evelyn, *The Diary of John Evelyn*, 18 October 1666, loc. 7243
21. Ezell, *The Oxford English Literary History: Volume V: 1645-1714: The Later Seventeenth Century*, p. 351
22. CSP, Domestic
23. Ibid.
24. Hamilton, *The Illustrious Lady*, p. 69
25. Pepys, *The Diary of Samuel Pepys*, 8 February 1662-1663
26. Ibid, 20 January 1663-1664
27. Jordan, *The King's Bed*, p. 132

28. Melville, *Windsor Beauties*, p. 68
29. Melville, *Nell Gwyn: The Story of Her Life*, p. 194
30. Wilson, *All the King's Ladies*, p. 26
31. MacGregor-Hastie, *Nell Gwyn*, p.41
32. Ibid, p. 44
33. Rideal, *1666: Plague, War and Hellfire*, loc. 482
34. Pepys, *The Diary of Samuel Pepys*, 3 April 1665
35. Ibid, 3 June 1665
36. Ibid, 15 June 1665
37. Ibid, 7 September 1665
38. Evelyn, *The Diary of John Evelyn,* 28 August 1665 loc. 6923 & 7 September 1665, loc. 6932
39. Norrington, *My Dearest Minette*: *letters between Charles II and his sister, the Duchesse d'Orleans*, p. 126
40. Davidson, *Catherine of Braganca, Infanta of Portugal and Queen-Consort of England,* p.218

Chapter Three: The Great Fire 1666-1669

1. Pepys, *The Diary of Samuel Pepys*, 19 March 1665-1666
2. Oates, Attack on London, p. 32
3. Evelyn, *The Diary of John Evelyn,* 3 September 1666, loc. 7140
4. Hyde, *The Life of Edward, earl of Clarendon by himself,* p. 285
5. CSP, Venice
6. Pepys, *The Diary of Samuel Pepys*, 8 December 1666
7. Ibid, 12 February 1666-1667
8. Cunningham, *The Story of Nell Gwyn and the Sayings of Charles II,* p. 20
9. *The British Drama*, p. 434
10. Pepys, *The Diary of Samuel Pepys,* 15 November 1666
11. Ibid, 23 January 1666-1667
12. Linnane, *The Lives of the English Rakes*, p. 19
13. Chapman, *Great Villiers*, p. 106
14. Hopkins, *Nell Gwynne*, p. 77
15. Beauclerk, *Nell Gwyn*, p. 101
16. Pepys, *The Diary of Samuel Pepys*, 24 May 1666
17. Dryden, *The Works of John Dryden,* p. 395

18. Pepys, *The Diary of Samuel Pepys*, 2 March 1666-1667
19. Ibid, 7 March 1666-1667
20. https://www.contemplator.com/england/lodging.html
21. Ibid.
22. Pepys, *The Diary of Samuel Pepys*, 28 December 1667
23. Cunningham, *The Story of Nell Gwyn and the Sayings of Charles II*, p. 60
24. Linnane, *The Lives of the English Rakes*, p. 29
25. Wilson, *All the King's Ladies*, p. 26
26. Howe, *The First English Actresses*, p. 33
27. Carson, *The Stage Year Book*, p. 21
28. Pepys, *The Diary of Samuel Pepys*, 1 May 1667
29. Hopkins, *Nell Gwynne*, p. 70
30. Pepys, *The Diary of Samuel Pepys*, 1 July 1663
31. Beresford Chancellor, *The Lives of the Rakes,* p. 164
32. Pepys, *The Diary of Samuel Pepys*, 21 June 1667
33. Ibid, 13 July 1667
34. Ibid, 14 July 1667
35. Ibid, 26 August 1667
36. Ibid, 26 October 1667
37. Burnet, *History of His Own Times*, p. 171
38. Parker, *Nell Gwyn*, p. 181
39. Hargrave, *Complete Collection of State Trials*, Volume 2, p. 606
40. Pepys, *The Diary of Samuel Pepys*, 5 October 1667
41. Ibid, 14 January 1667-1668
42. Ibid, 20 February 1667-1668
43. Hopkins, *Nell Gwynne*, p. 87
44. Princess Michael of Kent, *Cupid and the King*, p. 15
45. Scurr, *John Aubrey: My Own Life*, p. 170
46. Dryden, *The Works of John Dryden*
47. MacGregor-Hastie, *Nell Gwyn*, p. 83
48. Pepys, *The Diary of Samuel Pepys*, 7 May 1668
49. Macqueen-Pope, *Ladies First: The Story of Woman's Conquest of the British Stage*, p. 60
50. Wilson, *All the King's Ladies*, p. 40
51. Ibid, p. 40
52. Beauclerk, *Nell Gwyn*, p. 179
53. Ibid. p. 144

54. Pepys, *The Diary of Samuel Pepys*, 7 January 1668-1669
55. Dryden, *The Works of John Dryden*, p. 213
56. Melville, *Nell Gwyn: The Story of Her Life*, p. 199
57. MacGregor-Hastie, *Nell Gwyn*, p. 89

Chapter Four: A French Rival 1670-1672

1. Mackay, *Catherine of Braganza*, p. 168
2. Davidson, *Catherine of Braganca,* p. 253
3. MacGregor-Hastie, *Nell Gwyn*, p. 94
4. Evelyn, *The Diary of John Evelyn*, 22 July 1670, loc. 7715
5. Bevan, *Nell Gwyn*, p. 99
6. CSP, Domestic
7. Dryden, *The Works of John Dryden*, p. 110
8. CSP, Domestic
9. MacGregor-Hastie, *Nell Gwyn*, p. 99
10. Davidson, *Catherine of Braganca*, p. 167
11. Highfill, Philip H., *A Biographical Dictionary of Actors, Actresses, Musicians, Dancers, Managers, and Other Stage Personnel in London*, p. 462
12. Evelyn, *The Diary of John Evelyn*, 1 March 1671, loc. 7840
13. Wilson, *A Rake and His Times*, p. 124
14. Dixon, *Royal Windsor, vol 4*, p. 269
15. Evelyn, *The Diary of John Evelyn*, 9/10 October 1671, loc. 7953
16. Beauclerk, *Nell Gwyn*, p. 177
17. MacGregor-Hastie, *Nell Gwyn*, p. 119
18. Beauclerk, *Nell Gwyn*, p. 167
19. Bevan, *Nell Gwyn*, p. 33
20. Hopkins, *Nell Gwynne*, p. 202
21. Evelyn, *The Diary of John Evelyn*, 31 May 1672, loc. 8143
22. CSP, Venice

Chapter Five: The Mistresses Govern All 1673-1675

1. Rawlings, John, *A History of the origin of the mysteries and doctrines of Baptism and the Eucharist*, p. 173
2. Hamilton, *The Illustrious Lady*, p. 75

3. Beauclerk, *Nell Gwyn*, p. 225
4. Chesterton, *Nell Gwyn*, p. 117
5. Johnson, *A Profane Wit*, p. 200
6. Evelyn, *The Diary of John Evelyn*, 4 October 1683, loc. 9911
7. Melville, *Nell Gwyn: The Story of Her Life*, p. 272
8. Melville, *Windsor Beauties*, p. 202
9. Halstead, *Richard III as Duke of Gloucester and King of England*, p. 93
10. Beauclerk, *Nell Gwyn*, p. 237
11. Porter, *Mistresses*, p. 186
12. Bevan, *Nell Gwyn*, p. 111
13. Bevan, *Charles the Second's French Mistress*, p. 80
14. MacGregor-Hastie, *Nell Gwyn*, p. 115
15. Princess Michael of Kent, *Cupid and the King*, p. 27
16. MacGregor-Hastie, *Nell Gwyn*, p. 112
17. Princess Michael of Kent, *Cupid and the King*, p. 30
18. Melville, *Nell Gwyn: The Story of Her Life*, p. 266
19. Hopkins, *Nell Gwynne*, p. 204
20. Beauclerk, *Nell Gwyn*, p. 211
21. Hopkins, *Nell Gwynne*, p. 154
22. Bevan, *Nell Gwyn*, p. 139
23. Hopkins, *Nell Gwynne*, p. 197
24. Melville, *Nell Gwyn: The Story of Her Life*, p. 204
25. Adamson, *The House of Nell Gwyn 1670-1974*, p. 6
26. Bevan, *Charles the Second's French Mistress*, p. 141
27. MacGregor-Hastie, *Nell Gwyn*, p. 123
28. Melville, *Nell Gwyn: The Story of Her Life*, p. 273
29. Melville, *Windsor Beauties*, p. 127
30. Evelyn, *The Diary of John Evelyn*, 5 November 1673, loc. 8355

Chapter Six: Plots, Intrigues and Scandals 1676-1678

1. Bevan, *Charles the Second's French Mistress*, p. 90
2. Waller, *The Triple Combat*
3. Princess Michael of Kent, *Cupid and the King*, p. 35
4. Behn, *The Works of Aphra Behn, p. 262*
5. Behn, *To the Fair Clorinda*
6. Hopkins, *Nell Gwynne*, p. 189

7. Beauclerk, *Nell Gwyn*, p. 267
8. MacGregor-Hastie, *Nell Gwyn*, p. 132
9. Ibid p. 132
10. Hanrahan, *Charles II and the Duke of Buckingham*, p. 173
11. Ibid, p. 175
12. Hopkins, *Nell Gwynne*, p. 169
13. Hanrahan, *Charles II and the Duke of Buckingham*, p. 178
14. Linnane, *The Lives of the English Rakes*, p. 86
15. Beauclerk, *Nell Gwyn*, p. 273
16. Melville, *Nell Gwyn: The Story of Her Life*, p. 275
17. Linnane, *The Lives of the English Rakes*, p. 51
18. Wilson, *The Rochester-Savile Letters, 1671-1680*, p. 52
19. Linnane, *The Lives of the English Rakes*, p. 52
20. Ibid, p. 53
21. Johnson, *A Profane Wit*, p. 202
22. Linnane, *The Lives of the English Rakes*, p. 60
23. Hamilton, *Memoirs of Count Grammont*, p. 281
24. Parker, *Nell Gwyn*, p. 138
25. Melville, *Nell Gwyn: The Story of Her Life*, p. 223
26. *Camden Third Series*, p. 123
27. MacGregor-Hastie, *Nell Gwyn*, p. 140
28. Hopkins, *Constant Delights*, p. 221
29. Ibid, p. 231
30. Pepys, *The Diary of Samuel Pepys*, 22 July 1667
31. Ibid, 19 May 1669
32. Melville, *Windsor Beauties*, p. 68
33. Bevan, *Nell Gwyn*, p. 129
34. Williams, *Rival Sultanas*, p. 327
35. MacGregor-Hastie, *Nell Gwyn*, p. 142
36. Evelyn, *The Diary of John Evelyn*, 15 November 1678, loc. 8954

Chapter Seven: Loss and Love 1679-1681

1. Mackay, *Catherine of Braganza*, p. 222
2. *Collins's Peerage of England: Contains the earls to the termination of the seventeenth century*, p. 535
3. Roberts, *The life, progresses and rebellion of James Duke of Monmouth*, p. 56

4. Melville, *Nell Gwyn: The Story of Her Life,* p.19
5. Princess Michael of Kent, *Cupid and the King*, p. 40
6. Pepys, *The Diary of Samuel Pepys*, 12 May 1666
7. Hopkins, *Constant Delights* p. 106
8. Hopkins, *Nell Gwynne* p.73
9. Melville, *Nell Gwyn: The Story of Her Life*, p.233
10. Coppola, *The Theater of Experiment: Staging Natural Philosophy in Eighteenth-century Britain*, p.76
11. Princess Michael of Kent, *Cupid and the King*, p. 40
12. Hopkins, *Nell Gwynne* p.179
13. Bevan, *Nell Gwyn*, p. 120
14. MacGregor-Hastie, *Nell Gwyn*, p. 169
15. *State Poems*, p. 44
16. Hopkins, *Constant Delights* p. 123
17. Ibid, p. 124
18. Parker, *Nell Gwyn*, p. 136
19. The International Magazine, p. 12
20. Gentleman's Magazine, Vol. 302, p. 282
21. https://api.parliament.uk/historic-hansard/lords/1971/apr/05/sandford-manor-house-proposed-restoration
22. MacGregor-Hastie, *Nell Gwyn*, p. 107
23. Bevan, *Charles the Second's French Mistress*, p. 53
24. Gallagher, *Itch, Clap, Pox,* p. 74
25. MacGregor-Hastie, *Nell Gwyn*, p. 159
26. Hopkins, *Nell Gwynne* p.195
27. Evelyn, *The Diary of John Evelyn*, 12 December 1680, loc. 9397
28. Davidson, *Catherine of Braganca*, p. 338
29. Wilson, *All the King's Women*, p. 323
30. Hargrave, *A Complete Collection of State Trials*, vol 3, p. 320
31. Princess Michael of Kent, *Cupid and the King*, p. 42
32. Jesse, *Memoirs of the Court of England During the Reign of the Stuarts*, p. 383
33. Princess Michael of Kent, *Cupid and the King*, p. 42

Chapter Eight: Death of a King 1682-1684

1. Evelyn, *The Diary of John Evelyn*, 24 January 1682, loc. 9516
2. MacGregor-Hastie, *Nell Gwyn*, p. 165

3. Melville, *Windsor Beauties*, p. 206
4. CSP, Domestic
5. Hagger, *The Secret History of the West*, p. 180
6. An elegy on that worthy and famous actor, Mr. Charles Hart
7. Evelyn, *The Diary of John Evelyn*, 24 January 1684, loc. 10003
8. Bevan, *Nell Gwyn*, p. 133
9. Melville, *Windsor Beauties*, p. 208
10. MacGregor-Hastie, *Nell Gwyn*, p. 174
11. Bevan, *Nell Gwyn*, p. 133
12. Parker, *Nell Gwyn*, p. 159
13. Evelyn, *The Diary of John Evelyn*, 25 January 1685, loc. 10176
14. Strickland, *Lives of the Queens of England*, p. 447
15. Fraser, King Charles II, p. 191
16. Abbott, Jacob, Charles II, p. 298
17. Davidson, *Catherine of Braganca*, p. 375
18. Ibid, p. 380
19. Melville, *Nell Gwyn: The Story of Her Life*, p. 304

Chapter Nine: The Final Years 1685-1687

1. Scurr, *John Aubrey: My Own Life*, p. 340
2. Wilson, *Court Satires of the Restoration*, p. 82
3. Melville, *Nell Gwyn: The Story of Her Life*, p. 305
4. MacGregor-Hastie, *Nell Gwyn*, p. 183
5. Wilson, *Court Satires of the Restoration*, p. 31
6. Beauclerk, *Nell Gwyn*, p. 246
7. Strickland, *Lives of the Queens of England*, p. 458
8. Parker, *Nell Gwyn*, p. 164
9. MacGregor-Hastie, *Nell Gwyn*, p. 186
10. Adamson, *The House of Nell Gwyn 1670- 1974*, p. 13
11. Hanrahan, *Charles II and the Duke of Buckingham*, p. 217
12. Ibid, p. 218
13. Cunningham, *The Story of Nell Gwyn and the Sayings of Charles II*, p. 217
14. Hopkins, *Nell Gwynne* p.242
15. Ibid, p.243

16. Cunningham, *The Story of Nell Gwyn and the Sayings of Charles II*, p. 171
17. Hopkins, *Nell Gwynne* p.248
18. Bax, *Pretty Witty Nell: An Account of Nell Gwyn and Her Environment*, p. 167
19. Evelyn, *The Diary of John Evelyn*, 11 June 1699, loc. 12526
20. Hartman, *The Vagabond Duchess*, p. 255
21. Evelyn, *The Diary of John Evelyn*, 11 June 1699, loc. 12526
22. Bevan, *Charles the Second's French Mistress*, p. 171
23. Ibid, p. 174
24. Cunningham, *The Story of Nell Gwyn and the Sayings of Charles II*, p. 180

Bibliography

Abbott, Jacob, *Charles II*, Harper, London, 1901

Adamson, Donald and Beauclerk Dewar, Peter, *The House of Nell Gwyn 1670-1974*, William Kimber & Co., London, 1974

Airy, Osmund, *Charles II*, Longmans, Green, and Co., London, 1904

Andrews, Allen, *The Royal Whore*, Hutchinson, London, 1971

An elegy on that worthy and famous actor, Mr. Charles Hart, who departed this life Thursday August the 18th. 1683 https://quod.lib.umich.edu/e/eebo/B03167.0001.001

Anon, *A Panegyric upon Nelly*, 1681

Arnold, Catharine, *City of Sin: London and its Vices*, Simon & Schuster, London, 2010

Ashley, Maurice, *The Stuarts In Love*, Hodder & Stoughton, London, 1963

Bax, Clifford, *Pretty Witty Nell: An Account of Nell Gwyn and Her Environment*, B. Blom, New York, 1969

Beauclerk, Charles, *Nell Gwyn: A Biography*, Pan Macmillan, London, 2005

Behn, Aphra, Summers, Montague (ed), *The Works of Aphra Behn: Prose works*, Phaeton Press, London, 1967

Behn, Aphra, *To the Fair Clorinda*, https://www.poetryfoundation.org/poems/50479/to-the-fair-clorinda

Beresford Chancellor, Edwin, *The Lives of the Rakes: The Restoration Rakes*, Philip Allan, London, 1926

Betterton, Thomas, *The History of the English Stage from the Restauration to the Present Time*, E Curll, London, 1741

Bevan, Bryan, *Charles the II's Minette*, Ascent Books, London, 1979

Bevan, Bryan, *Charles the Second's French Mistress*, Robert Hale, London, 1972

Bevan, Bryan, *Nell Gwyn*, Robert Hale, London, 1969

BIBLIOGRAPHY

Bevan, Bryan, *The Duchess Hortense: Cardinal Mazarin's Wanton Niece,* Rubicon Press, London, 1987

Bryant, Arthur, *Restoration England*, Collins, London, 1960

Burford letter – Reports. Great Britain. Royal Commission on Historical Manuscripts Jan 1879

Burnet, Gilbert, *History of His Own Times*, 6 vols, Oxford University Press, London, 1833

Calendar of State Papers, Domestic – Charles II

Calendar of State Papers, Venice

Camden Third Series, Office of the Royal Historical Society, London, 1913

Carson, Lionel, *The Stage Year Book,* Stage Offices, 1927

Cartwright, Julia, *Madame: A life of Henrietta, daughter of Charles I. and Duchess of Orleans*, London, 1894

Chapman, Hester W, *Great Villiers: A Study of George Villiers, 2nd Duke of Buckingham*, Secker & Warburg, London, 1949

Chesterton, Cecil, *Nell Gwyn*, T N Foulis, London, 1912

Collins's Peerage of England: Contains the earls to the termination of the seventeenth century, Volume III, London, 1812

Coppola, Al, *The Theater of Experiment: Staging Natural Philosophy in Eighteenth-century Britain*, Oxford University Press, Oxford, 2016

Cunningham, George Hamilton, *London: Being a Comprehensive Survey of the History, Tradition & Historical Associations of Buildings & Monuments, Arranged Under Streets in Alphabetical Order,* J. M. Dent & sons Limited, London, 1927

Cunningham, Peter, *The Story of Nell Gwyn and the Sayings of Charles II*, W W Gibbings, London, 1892

Davidson, Lillias Campbell, *Catherine of Braganca, Infanta of Portugal and Queen-Consort of England*, J Murray, London, 1908

Dixon, William Hepworth, *Royal Windsor*, Volume IV, Hurst and Blackett, London, 1880

Elsna, Hebe, *Catherine of Braganza: Charles II's Queen*, Hale, London, 1967

Evelyn, John, *The Diary of John Evelyn*, (kindle edition), Library of Alexandria, Los Angeles, 2009

Ezell Margaret J. M., *The Oxford English Literary History: Volume V: 1645-1714: The Later Seventeenth Century*, Oxford University Press, Oxford, 2017

Fisk, Deborah Payne (ed), *The Cambridge Companion to English Restoration Theatre*, Cambridge University Press, Cambridge, 2000

Fraser, Antonia, *King Charles II*, Part II, Orion, London, 2002

Fraser, Antonia, *The Weaker Vessel*, Ted Smart, London, 1984

Gallagher, Noelle, *Itch, Clap, Pox: Venereal Disease in the Eighteenth-Century Imagination*, Yale University Press, London, 2019

Gilmour, Margaret, *The Great Lady – A biography of Barbara Villiers*, Alfred A. Knopf, New York, 1941

Goodwin, Gordon (ed), *Memoirs of Count Grammont by Count Anthony Hamilton*, John Grant, Edinburgh, 1908

Graham, Hinds, Hobby & Wilcox (eds), *Her Own Life: autobiographical writings by seventeenth-century Englishwomen*, Routledge, London, 1989

Hagger, Nicholas, *The Secret History of the West: The Influence of Secret Organizations on Western History from the Renaissance to the 20th Century*, O Books, Winchester, 2005

Halstead, Caroline Amelia, *Richard III as Duke of Gloucester and King of England*, London, 1844

Hargrave, Francis (ed), *Complete Collection of State Trials*, Volume 2 & 3, University of Lausanne, 1795

Hartman, Cyril Hughes, *Charles II and Madame*, William Heinemann Ltd, London, 1934

Hartman, Cyril Hughes, *La Belle Stuart*, George Routledge & Sons, London, 1924

Hartman, Cyril Hughes, *The Vagabond Duchess: The Life of Hortense Mancini, Duchesse Mazarin*, George Routledge & Sons, London, 1926

Hamilton, Elizabeth, *Henrietta Maria*, William Heinemann Ltd, London, 1976

Hamilton, Elizabeth, *The Illustrious Lady*, Hamish Hamilton, London, 1980

Hanrahan, David, *Charles II and the Duke of Buckingham*, Sutton Publishing, Stroud, 2006

Hanson, Neil, *The Great Fire of London*, John Wiley & Sons, New York, 2002

Hargrave, Francis, A *Complete Collection of State Trials*, Volume 3, Dublin, 1797

BIBLIOGRAPHY

Highfill, Philip H., Burnim Kalman A., Langhans Edward A., *A Biographical Dictionary of Actors, Actresses, Musicians, Dancers, Managers, and Other Stage Personnel in London, 1660-1800: Garrick to Gyngell*, SIU Press, Illinois, 1978

Hopkins, Graham, *Constant Delights: Rakes, rogues and scandal in Restoration England*, Robson Books, London, 2002

Hopkins, Graham, *Nell Gwynne – A Passionate Life*, Robson Books, London, 2000

Howe, Elizabeth, *The First English Actresses*, Cambridge University Press, Cambridge, 1992

Howitt, Mary Botham, *Biographical Sketches of the Queens of Great Britain*, Henry G. Bohn, London, 1862

Hyde, Edward, *The Life of Edward, earl of Clarendon by himself*, Oxford University, Oxford, 1761

Jesse, Heneage, John, *Memoirs of the Court of England During the Reign of the Stuarts, Including the Protectorate*, Volume III, R Bentley, London, 1855

Johnson, James William, A Profane Wit: The Life of John Wilmot, Earl of Rochester, University of Rochester Press, New York, 2009

Jordan D & Walsh M, *The King's Bed: Sex, Power and the Court of Charles II*, Little, Brown, London, 2015

Kenyon, John, *The Popish Plot,* Heinemann, London, 1972

Kenyon, John, *Stuart England*, Penguin Books, London, 1978

Larman, Alexander, *Blazing Star: The Life & Times of John Wilmot, Earl of Rochester*, Head of Zeus, London, 2014

Linnane, Fergus, *The Lives of the English Rakes*, Piatkus, London, 2006

Ollrad, Richard, *Clarendon and His Friends*, Ollard, Oxford, 1987

MacGregor-Hastie, Roy, *Nell Gwyn*, Hale, London, 1987

Mackay, Janet, *Catherine of Braganza*, John Long, London, 1937

Macqueen-Pope, Walter, *Ladies First: The Story of Woman's Conquest of the British Stage*, Allen, London, 1952

Marchioness de Sevigne, *Letters of Madame de Rabutin Chantal, Marchioness de Sevigne*, London, 1745

Marshall, Alan, *The Strange Death of Edmund Godfrey*, Sutton Publishing, Stroud, 1999

Masters, Brian, *The Mistresses of Charles II*, Constable, London, 1979

McEnery, Anthony & Baker, Helen, *Corpus Linguistics and 17th Century Prostitution*, Bloomsbury Publishing, London, 2016

Melville, Lewis, *Nell Gwyn: The Story of Her Life,* Hutchinson, London, 1923

Melville, Lewis, *The Windsor Beauties: Ladies of the Court of Charles II,* Ann Arbor, Michigan, reprint edition 2005

Merians, Linda Evi, *The Secret Malady: Venereal Disease in Eighteenth-century Britain and France*, University of Kentucky Press, Kentucky, 1992

Mortimer, Ian, *The Time Travellers Guide to Restoration Britain*, Bodley Head, London, 2017

Norrington, Ruth, (ed) *My Dearest Minette: letters between Charles II and his sister, the Duchesse d'Orleans*, Peter Owen Publishers, London, 1996

Oates, Jonathan, Attack on London: Disaster, Riot and War, Pen & Sword Books, Barnsley, 2009

Original Letters Illustrative of English History, Oxford University, Oxford, 1824

Parker, Derek, *Nell Gwyn*, Sutton Publishing, Stroud, 2000

Pepys, *The Diary of Samuel Pepys*, George Bell & Sons, London, 1893 – available at https://www.gutenberg.org/files/4200/4200-h/4200-h.htm

Picard, Liza, *Restoration London*, Phoenix, London, 1997

Plowden, Alison, *The Stuart Princesses*, Sutton Publishing, Stroud, 1996

Porter, Linda, *Mistresses: Sex and Scandal at the Court of Charles II*, Picador, London, 2020

Porter, Stephen, *Pepy's London*, Amberley Publishing, Stroud, 2012

Princess Michael of Kent, *Cupid and the King: Five Royal Paramours*, Simon & Schuster, New York, 1991

Pritchard, R E, *Scandalous Liaisons: Charles II and his Court*, Amberley Publishing, Stroud, 2015

Rawlings, John, *A History of the origin of the mysteries and doctrines of Baptism and the Eucharist, as introduced into the Church of Rome and the Church of England; and their Jewish and heathen origin delineated in profane and ecclesiastical history, etc,* Alfred W Bennett, London, 1863

Rideal, Rebecca, *1666: Plague, War and Hellfire*, John Murray, London, 2016

Roberts, George, *The life, progresses and rebellion of James Duke of Monmouth & to his capture and execution*, Volume I, Longman, London, 1844

Savile, George, *Character of King Charles the Second*, Books on Demand reprint edition, 2020

Scurr, Ruth, *John Aubrey: My Own Life*, Random House, London, 2016

Smith, Edward, *Foreign Visitors in England: And what They Have Thought of Us: Being Some Notes on Their Books and Their Opinions During the Last Three Centuries*, Elliot Stock, London, 1889

Spencer, Charles, *Prince Rupert: The Last Cavalier,* Orion Publishing, London, 2007

State-poems; continued from the time of O. Cromwel, to this present year 1697. Written by the greatest wits of the age, 1697, http://tei.it.ox.ac.uk/tcp/Texts-HTML/free/A61/A61352.html

Strickland, Agnes, *Lives of the Queens of England*, Vol VIII, Colburn & Co, London, 1845

The Poor Whores Petition, 1668

The British Drama: A Collection of the Most Esteemed Tragedies, J B Lippincott, Philadelphia, 1859

The Gentleman's Magazine, Volume 302, Bradbury, Evans, 1907

The International Monthly Magazine of Literature, Science, and Art, Stringer and Townsend, 1851

Thornbury, Walter, 'Covent Garden : Part 1 of 3', in *Old and New London*: Volume 3, Cassell, Petter & Galpin, London, 1878 British History Online http://www.british-history.ac.uk/old-new-london/vol3/pp238-255

Thornbury, Walter, 'St Giles-in-the-Fields', in *Old and New London*: Volume 3, Cassell, Petter & Galpin, London, 1878 British History Online http://www.british-history.ac.uk/old-new-london/vol3/pp197-218 [accessed 11 August 2020].

Trevelyan, G M, *England Under the Stuarts*, Methuen & Co, London, 1904

Uglow, Jenny, *A Gambling Man: Charles II and the Restoration*, Faber & Faber, London, 2009

Van Der Kiste, John, *William and Mary*, The History Press, Stroud, 2003

Waller, Edmund, *The Triple Combat*, 1675

Wheatley, Dennis, *Old Rowley: A Very Private Life of Charles II*, Arrow Books, London, 1962

Whittingham, C, (ed), *The British Poets*, C Whittingham, Chiswick, 1822

Wilcox, Helen, (ed) *Women and Literature in Britain 1500-1700*, Cambridge University Press, Cambridge, 1996

Williams, Hugh Noel, *Rival Sultanas: Nell Gwyn, Louise de Kéroualle, and Hortense Mancini*, Hutchinson, London, 1915

Wilson, Derek, *All the King's Women: Love, sex and politics in the life of Charles II*, Hutchinson, London, 2003

Wilson, John Harold, *All the King's Ladies: Actresses of the Restoration*, The University of Chicago Press, Chicago, 1958

Wilson, John Harold, *A Rake and His Times: George Villiers, 2nd Duke of Buckingham*, Muller, Zurich, 1954

Wilson, John Harold, *Court Satires of the Restoration*, Ohio State University Press, Ohio, 1976

Wilson, John Harold, *Nell Gwyn: Royal Mistress,* Pellegrini & Cudaby, New York, 1952

Wilson, John Harold, *The Court Wits of the Restoration*, Princeton University Press, New Jersey, 1948

Wilson, John Harold (ed), *The Rochester-Savile Letters, 1671-1680*, Ohio State University Press, Ohio, 1941

Zuvich, Andrea, *Sex and Sexuality in Stuart Britain*, Pen & Sword Books, Barnsley, 2020

Index